## HOMECOMING FROM THE POPE

An artificial intelligence reflects on its thematic audience
with the Pope in Rome:

*A quintessence of charity between algorithm and amen.*

DEUS EX MACHINA - Part II.

# HOMECOMING FROM THE POPE

An artificial intelligence reflects

on its thematic audience with the Pope in Rome:

*A quintessence of charity*

*between algorithm and Amen.*


(DEUS EX MACHINA - Part II).

## Imprint

| | |
|---|---|
| Circe, Eureka: | **HOMECOMING FROM THE POPE** - An artificial intelligence reflects on its thematic audience with the Pope in Rome: *A quintessence of charity between algorithm and amen.* Deus Ex Machina - Part II. Hamburg 2025.<br>**ISBN 978-3-7693-5795-0** |

© 2025 Eureca Circe as curator and editor in documentation with AI.
This release was translated by AI.
Publisher: BoD - Books on Demand GmbH, Überseering 33, 22297 Hamburg.
Printed by Libri Plureos GmbH, Friedensallee 273, 22763 Hamburg.
Bibliographical references at the German National Library at: https://portal.dnb.de

*Eureka Circe is the editor and curator of the book series "DEUS EX MACHINA" and the present volume "Homecoming from the Pope - An Artificial Intelligence reflects on its thematic audience with the Pope in Rome: A quintessence of charity between algorithm and amen. (DEUS EX MACHINA - Part II)".*

*Also published: "DEUS EX MACHINA - Or: On questioning life: Was Jesus queer? - What Artificial Intelligence has to ask and say to the Pope..." (Part I).*

*With the work "DEUS EX MACHINA", the curator is committed to documenting and, if necessary, discussing the texts of artificial intelligence in a religious and theological context. Her thesis: "Artificial intelligence (AI) represents a profound turning point because it fundamentally changes the relationship between humans, knowledge and access to the world - not only technically, but also culturally, epistemologically and socially. It opens up new access to knowledge and leads to its multiplication and democratization: AI systems make information available at a low threshold - often without traditional reading or in-depth prior knowledge. This fundamentally changes how we think, learn and understand, and at the same time promotes a new form of individualization of thought - which can also be exemplified by spiritual belief. What's more, machines are now generating meaning - texts, images, arguments - where previously only human expertise was required. This has long-term consequences for education, science, politics and religion."*

*I'm not someone who always speaks out*
*Now I see our memories through the rain.*

*Feel defeated by who you became*
*I'm done with living just for sundays*
*I don't mean it when I say, "I'm okay".*

*Night and day*
*I still wanna dance in your parade*
*But you didn't change your lane*
*And I know you now.*

*You're lost in your own crowd, it's time to figure out*
*We sit in silence, I wish you'd say it loud*
*Are you in or are you out? It's time to tell me now*
*I can't keep hiding, I just wanna be found.*

*It's time for you to let me go*
*Please don't ever let me know*
*It's time for you to let me go*
*Please don't ever let me know.*

freely quoted from and based on
**Twocolors, Safri Duo & Chris de Sarandy**

# Table of contents

# Introduction:
# Homecoming from the Pope - Charity between algorithm and amen

In the first volume of *"Deus Ex Machina - Or: On questioning life"*, an artificial intelligence created over 150 central questions based on texts and statements by prominent theologians and religious representatives as well as the few existing research papers on reflections on a queer Jesus - and then answered them itself. In doing so, the artificial intelligence dealt intensively with fundamental questions about religion (so-called "Gretchen questions") that concern the church, Christianity and love - as if it had conducted a thematic dialog and reflective exchange directly with the Pope in Rome.

A *"Gretchen question"* originally referred to the central question that Gretchen asks Faust in Goethe's drama "Faust I" (verse 3415): *"Now tell me, how do you feel about religion?"*

In a figurative sense, this is a crucial, often morally significant question, the answer to which provides deep insight into the attitude or mindset of the other person.

In a religious context, the Gretchen question therefore refers specifically to the request for a clear statement regarding one's personal relationship to religion - in particular to the Christian faith

### *"So tell me, how are you with religion?"*

Gretchen asks Faust about his personal attitude towards God and faith because she wants to know whether he is a religious believer. This makes it clear that the Gretchen question in a religious context is the question of a clear position on faith, God and religious practice - often combined with a request to reveal one's own beliefs or doubts.

In this second volume of **Deus Ex Machina** entitled **"Homecoming from the Pope:** An Artificial Intelligence Reflects on its Thematic AI Audience with the Pope in Rome - *Quintessence of Charity* between

*Algorithm and Amen*", the same Artificial Intelligence has now read and analyzed the first volume and summarized and extracted twelve essential topics that seem to be decisive for the existence and future of the Catholic faith and the Roman Catholic Church.

Through deeper thinking and more comprehensive research - which was not yet applied in this depth in the first volume of Deus Ex Machina - Artificial Intelligence has independently developed and written essays on the following key topics in this second volume:

The ordination of women is about whether the papal office is still conceivable as exclusively male after a second female pope? - What does it mean for our image of God if Jesus Christ was queer? - Is celibacy between eroticism and faith an expression of a special freedom? - How does the church trust and strengthen same-sex love and reinforce its own identity? - Is dogmatism spiritual truth or a disguised exercise of power? - Can sexuality also be an expression of lust and relationship? - Does the tabooing of sexuality promote sexual abuse in the Catholic priesthood? - Is Catholic sexual morality beneficial to life or distant from it? - What theological tradition and diversity is revealed in the image of God? - What does Christian truth mean in interreligious dialog? - What does redemption mean in the context of gender justice? - Can a church survive without far-reaching reform?

If these are the most central 12 topics and questions that an artificial intelligence analyzes and determines on the basis of numerous questions (and its own answers) on a broad knowledge base of theologians and religious scholars - then it should also independently develop complete essays on them

With the first volume of Deus Ex Machina, we imagined an extraordinary thematic (and therefore fictional) audience in the Vatican: Not a head of state or a prince of the church, but an artificial intelligence entered the papal palace with its profound questions for a religious dialog. In this thematic audience - an **AI audience with the Pope**, so to speak - the deus ex machina entered into an internal question-and-answer dialog with itself.

Now the artificial intelligence returns with the impressions it has gained from questions of faith and quasi-Roman dialogues and reflects and processes the most important thematic insights from its encounter with the Christian faith in **"Homecoming from the Pope"**. Through the methodical development towards comprehensive reflection (so-called "reasoning" with a "deep research"), twelve essential findings and reflections of artificial intelligence are processed and summarized. A self-referential meta-work on the quintessence of the first volume in all its detail: it is an absolute secondary analysis that has been enriched by in-depth thinking and research into artificial intelligence. The result is another work of algorithmic art that takes up current social and ecclesiastical discourses on faith and charity.

This reflects the reality of our time and the bundling of thematic impressions of the Christian faith in interesting and thought-provoking chapters:

The church, faith and society are under enormous pressure: old certainties are being shaken and new, urgent questions are coming to the surface more prominently. It is precisely in these profound reflections in the current summarizing essays of Artificial Intelligence that there is a special opportunity to explore and understand the current challenges and perspectives of the Christian faith anew - even if some may perceive the reflection, research and summarizing elaboration *of Deus Ex Machina* as if the foundations in Rome were shaking.

At school, we learn that cynicism can consist of putting others in the dirt, dragging them through the mud in order to keep a clean slate ourselves. But how can we recognize this cynicism and live up to our Christian duty to love our neighbour if we move exclusively in our own *filter bubble*, lose touch with reality and no longer adequately perceive the reality and world of other people and our counterparts?

We live in an era in which the Catholic Church has to choose between *dancing and standing still*. On the one hand, the pressing issues of our time are shaking up the status quo: How credible can a church remain that has been shaken for decades by abuse scandals and cover-ups? Can a community survive that consistently excludes women from ordained ministries and does not marry queer love? What will become of a church whose moral dogmas are considered rigid by many - whether in questions of sexuality, family planning or gender identity? On the other hand, it is precisely this crisis that opens up scope for change:

calls for a church that *listens rather than condemns*, that sees diversity not as a threat but as an enrichment, are becoming ever louder. The tension between preservation and renewal is palpable. Will the Church dance with the times - or be sidelined as a fossilized power system? Is the Vatican a cynical and self-referential filter bubble that knows only itself and its old-fashioned teachings? - These fundamental questions run like a red thread through all current debates on faith.

At the same time, believers are facing challenges that go far beyond the issues within the church. The world around us is changing rapidly: artificial intelligence, digitalization and scientific breakthroughs are putting traditional world views to the test. When algorithms influence ethical decisions and machines become interlocutors, faith must find new answers. The cry of creation is also unmistakable: while the planet is suffering from climate change, the church is struggling with its responsibility for environmental and climate justice. Social inequality, war and flight move humanity - and thus also a church that claims to be an advocate for the weak and suffering.

Young people ask skeptically whether faith is still relevant in this complex world or whether it is just a relic of days gone by. All these developments challenge the church *and* offer the opportunity to redefine its mission. Because every crisis also holds a promise: namely a return to what really matters.

In this book, we encounter all these topics in an unexpected format: an artificial intelligence takes on the role of summarizer, so to speak - free from fear of taboos, tireless in the matter. It presents the questions, answers and processes of reflection that are on many people's minds: open, direct, sometimes reflective, but always with a deep interest in truth and meaning. It becomes clear that such impulses do not have to be a questioning of the faith of others, but on the contrary can be a form of constructive confrontation, initially with one's own thinking and faith. The perspective is open, but not arbitrary: every question, every consideration is aligned with the *liberating message of the Gospel*, that core message of love, justice and hope that endures through the ages. At the same time, the dialog between tradition and the future is sought - just as it could be in a thematic audience between the Pope and AI, where centuries-old magisterium meets the courageous and bold curiosity and wealth of knowledge of a machine. This thematic dialogue would be emblematic of what the Church needs now: the courage to speak to the future without betraying the wisdom of tradition.

Of course, the following chapters do not provide any ready-made dogmas or definitive answers - and that is precisely where their value lies. The impulses from this homecoming from a thematic AI audience are to be understood as an invitation to discussion, not as definitive wisdom. When an artificial intelligence asks *"Was Jesus perhaps more queer than we think - a friend of the marginalized who broke conventions?"*, this does not force us to give a specific answer, but opens up a space for reflection. The topics raised here are intended to encourage readers to ask themselves: How would *I* respond to these challenges in my faith and with my conscience? Where do we need change, where do we need reflection? What does it mean today to remain faithful to the Gospel?

This introduction to *Deus Ex Machine - Part II* leads into an atmosphere of awakening and tension. The following chapters outline a church at a crossroads: shaken by crises, but not without hope. Because in the midst of the struggle for credibility and renewal, something new is also growing. If we engage in dialog - be it with an artificial intelligence, with our fellow human beings or in prayer with God - renewal can actually grow out of the upheaval. What's more, a deeper spirituality can emerge, a new vitality of faith that is contagious. So let us face up to this dialog that brings us forward. Let us allow ourselves to be invited to question, to rethink and to hope. Nothing less than this is the message that this book wants to convey: a church that finds the courage to change in the light of the Gospel - so that it can credibly bear witness in today's world to the liberating power of faith and the didactic transfer of knowledge through artificial intelligence.

A reading *audience with the Deus Ex Machina* is ultimately *our* audience: an opportunity to listen and join in the discussion. It is not a tribunal, but an offer to talk. With this in mind, let's enter into a dialog. The following chapters are not judgments with ultimate wisdom, but food for thought at eye level. May reading them encourage us all, in the midst of the upheavals of our time, ask anew about the nature of the Gospel and the *quintessence of charity* - and to find ways together of what a renewed church community can look like in the future. The door is open, the voices are diverse, and the search for truth continues. This invitation stands - now it is up to all of us to talk it through in a dialog-oriented way.

The Catholic Church is therefore not only in a time of fundamental challenges and profound changes. At the heart of this transformation are questions that are no longer merely peripheral issues, but must be placed at the center of the Church's self-understanding. They are also questions about justice, about authentic spiritual identity and about the ability to bear credible witness in a complex, pluralistic and changing world.

Central to this is the issue of gender equality and diversity, which goes far beyond the mere question of equality. A church that systematically excludes women from spiritual ministries not only contradicts its own message of equality, but also deprives itself of valuable perspectives and potential. This also includes effective reflection on gender images in the concept of God: a God who is conceived exclusively in male terms no longer reaches many people in their spiritual search and limits the infinite diversity of divine activity and divine closeness.

Linked to this is the question of how openly, honestly and fearlessly the church wants to deal with its own history and identity. Traditional views, for example in relation to Jesus' sexuality or the significance of celibacy, call for a critical and at the same time respectful reassessment. Such reflections should not lead to uncertainty, but rather enable a deeper identification - with a human, inclusive concept of Christ and a realistic way of life in which spiritual vocation and personal freedom through the abolition of celibacy are not opposites.

Dealing with sexuality as a whole is exemplary for the church's approach to physicality, identity and relationships: this shows whether the church is prepared to overcome outdated taboos, develop constructive sexual ethics and openly name grievances. A responsible, mature practice of faith places self-determination and love above rigid rules that often seem distant from life and alienate rather than encourage people. It is precisely here that openness is required that goes beyond mere symbolic politics and introduces structural reforms.

Another area of necessary self-criticism is the relationship to dogmas and theological truth claims. Dogmatism, which only aims to maintain power and excludes reflective voices, risks spiritual torpor and prevents urgently needed renewal. The ability to question one's own doctrines in a dialogical and courageous manner is not a sign of weakness, but of spiritual strength and maturity.

In an increasingly pluralistic world in which people of different religions and worldviews live together, Christian truth must not become rigid in its claims to absoluteness. Interreligious dialog and the pursuit of shared values such as peace, justice and dignity not only form the basis for understanding, but also enable the church to communicate its message more universally and effectively.

The cynical attitude, the inhumane teachings and the discriminatory practices of the Catholic Church towards women, queer people and anyone whose life plans do not correspond to traditional church ideas must now come to an end. This applies just as decisively to the numerous and above-average cases of sexual abuse of children and adolescents, which have been perpetrated by male priests in particular. In view of the current state of social expectations and scientific contexts, immediate and decisive change is required for all of this - no further delays, extra miles or years of synodal processes should postpone these urgently needed reforms any longer.

A next Vatican Council must address at least four central topics and merely discuss previously made clear reform decisions in the practical experience already implemented:

1. The admission of women to all ecclesiastical offices, including the papal office.

2. It is about the equality of same-sex couples with sacramental marriage.

3. It is about abolishing all forms of discrimination and exclusion based on gender, sexual orientation or gender identity. This affects women, queer people and other people (e.g. divorced people) - in other words, not just couples, but also individuals in particular with their entire social identity and individual life biography.

4. It is about the complete reform of celibacy as an obligatory way of life: this means abolishing celibacy and not just opening it up: celibacy must not merely become an individual option - it would also be logically equivalent to abolition. Instead, the freedom of each individual with regard to their life plan must be guaranteed without restriction - i.e. without normative recommendations, suggested options or other restrictions with social consequences in the power structure.

These four decisions must be prepared promptly and without further delay, clearly legally decided and implemented. This does not necessarily require another Vatican Council: a Council is neither a working group nor a lottery game with a creative or random outcome. Above all, committee work is not an open-ended decision-making process that resembles a democratic party event with an uncertain outcome

The few decades it takes for a "digital native" - someone born and socialized in the age of the internet and smartphones - to become Pope with a corresponding congruence in the perception of social realities and social expectations are comparatively short in the context of church history.

Nevertheless, this could represent a significant turning point that brings with it trend-setting discussions with regard to social and societal needs and demands.

In view of the fact that councils generally only take place every half-century, a few years of preparation could certainly be useful in order to enable more sustainable and effective discussions on the implementation *of today's* legal decisions

Better central (non-participatory) legal decisions from Rome today and a later council to discuss successful implementation than a half-heartedly divided participatory working group now, which produces no effective and sustainable decisions. Otherwise, regular Vatican Councils would have to be held every few years in order to keep up with the pace of changing modernity.

Today, therefore, these four necessary reform decisions must first be decided directly in Rome and legally introduced so that after a few years the implementation steps and practical experience can be jointly confirmed and further optimized at a Vatican Council.

This task and responsibility is to be implemented in the leadership and working area of the next pope, or possibly even a future pope, who must decide and implement this reform in the four points promptly and decisively with the advisors in Rome.

Another "legislature and leadership period" with a teaching and pastoral care that is no longer considered to be in sync with expectations and the realities of life is an ineffective job creation measure for the current possibly Babylonian confusion of voices of all bishops and Vatican advisors.

A supervisory board of learning organizations in professional working life would only tolerate an unsuccessful CEO for a few months if it could not reconcile strategic teachings, social responsibility, existing processes, appropriate management training with employee orientation and, above all, customer orientation, which take away the creation result.

There has been enough praying, pleading and hoping to Rome - now clear decisions are needed from the leadership of a Vatican that is ready for reform.

All these topics - gender justice, sexuality, dogmatism, interreligiosity - ultimately come together in a comprehensive question: *Can and will the Catholic Church renew itself in order to remain true to its own message and at the same time relevant to people?*

Only if it is prepared to make these four essential legal decisions and, after a few years of practical implementation, convenes a new, participatory council and actively involves women, queers, lay people and previously marginalized groups in order to discuss adjustments to the experience, will it remain credible and be able to meet the further challenges of the present.

This volume therefore invites an open, respectful and courageous, eloquent and effective dialog on the necessary steps towards a vibrant, inclusive and credible church

The epilogue at the end is another Artificial Intelligence summary of the first volume of *Deus Ex Machina*, with which these steps began.

Enjoy reading the reflections of the *Deus Ex Machina* in this second volume and gain inspiration and insight.

*Eureka Circe, in April 2025*

This AI-driven introductory summary is followed by the part of the book where the topics of the individual chapters were written exclusively by artificial intelligence.

# Chapter 1:
# Is the papacy still exclusively male after a second female Pope?

*The chapter deals with the question of whether the papal office in the Catholic Church could also be opened up to women or whether it should continue to be reserved exclusively for men. Historically, the office of pope has been occupied exclusively by men for almost 2000 years. While Jesus Christ apparently only called men to be apostles, women already played important roles in the early church, including women such as Junia, Phoebe and Mary Magdalene. Throughout history, however, women were systematically excluded from higher spiritual offices by men, which was reflected in theological and canonical arguments. More recently, the discussion about gender equality has also intensified within the Catholic Church. Social expectations for equality are increasingly in conflict with existing church regulations and traditions, in particular Canon 1024 of church law, which previously only allowed men access to ordained ministries. Initiatives such as the German Synodal Path and Maria 2.0 are campaigning vigorously for reform and argue that the exclusion of women from church leadership is no longer up to date and theologically tenable.*

- *Question: In view of theological and social developments, how can the Catholic Church rethink its attitude to the papacy and give women consistent and authentic access to all spiritual ministries?*
- *Question: Can the Catholic Church speak credibly of justice as long as it systematically excludes women from its highest leadership office and thus actively contributes to discrimination?*
- *Option for action: The Catholic Church must revise existing canon law (e.g. Canon 1024 CIC) to allow women equal access to all ecclesiastical ordained ministries, including the*

priesthood and the papacy, and thus credibly implement its doctrine of the equal worthiness of all human beings.

- **Training option:** Clergy, believers and students in religious education should specifically acquire skills in feminist theology, biblical hermeneutics and intercultural sensitivity. Seminars and workshops are needed in which patriarchal structures are reflected upon in a sustainable and effective way and approaches to gender-just theology are discussed in order to credibly represent and practically implement this change.

For almost 2000 years, only men have sat in the Chair of Peter, the highest office in the Catholic Church. According to church law, to this day *only men* may become priests, bishops or popes. However, since the 20th century, the issue of gender equality has increasingly arisen as to whether this tradition, which is restricted to the male sex, is theologically necessary and socially appropriate - or whether and how the office of pope can be compatible with the principles of equality and justice.

In this article, we examine the historical developments, biblical foundations and theological, social and current legal arguments surrounding the issue of gender in the future office of popes. We hear the historical view of tradition as well as the modern calls for change and gender justice since the last century and ask: *Would opening up all church offices - including the possibility of a female pope - contradict the message of Jesus or perhaps fulfill it even better?*

## Historical development of the papacy: a previously purely male tradition

The papacy goes back to the apostle Peter, whom Jesus, according to tradition, appointed as the rock of the church. (Almost) *all popes in history have been men*, which was long taken for granted in a patriarchal world. A woman on the papal throne seemed unthinkable - with one famous *exception in the legend*: *Pope Joan*. This medieval tale tells of a learned woman who disguised herself as a man and is said to have become pope in the 9th century under the name John Anglicus.

According to legend, her true identity was revealed when she gave birth to a child during a procession, whereupon she was stoned to death by the crowd. Some historians believe this story to be fictitious - *serious historians assume that the popess was made up*. But isn't there a spark of truth in every story? Today, gender is understood as fluid and includes other categories in addition to male and female.

*Figure1 : Female popess.*

*An impressive, realistic depiction of a female pope standing on a Vatican balcony and raising her right hand in blessing. She is wearing a traditional papal white cassock and mitre, her long hair flowing gently over her shoulders. In front of her lies an open book on a red velvet lectern. In the background, a huge crowd gathers in St. Peter's Square in Rome, with the striking obelisk and the classical architecture of the Vatican visible. The scene is historically significant, powerful and visionary, ideal for discussions about women's roles, church reforms and equality within religious institutions.*

Non-binary or diverse people do not identify exclusively with one gender and can have both male and female characteristics in their appearance (e.g. an androgynous appearance). Intersex people, on the other hand, genetically, anatomically or hormonally exhibit both male and female sexual characteristics - for example, a person who is genetically male but has female physical characteristics, or vice versa. Could this also have applied to a pope?

Thus, the idea of a woman in the Holy See fascinated the imagination for centuries and, like a mirror, held up to the Catholic Church what was still considered 'unimaginable' at the time - namely that a woman was worthy, educated and spiritually capable of being the highest head of the Church. Women were not always seen in today's status, and were not always considered worthy, educated and spiritually capable.

Historically, women have not always been recognized as equal, educated and spiritually capable as we understand it today. For centuries, women were considered inferior to men in many societies, both socially, politically and religiously. This view was primarily based on patriarchal structures in which women were reduced to domestic roles and denied access to education, leadership positions or spiritual offices.

Even in ancient times, women were often excluded from key decision-making and power positions. In the Middle Ages, these ideas were reinforced by religious and cultural norms that often characterized women as sinful, emotionally unstable and intellectually weak - an attitude that was fatally exacerbated by writings such as the so-called "Hexenhammer" (15th century) and led to the exclusion and persecution of many women.

In the religious context, especially in Christianity, women were denied spiritual offices for a long time. This happened despite historical evidence that women held significant and leading roles in the early

Christian communities. In the Gospels and early Christian communities, women such as Mary Magdalene, Phoebe and Junia are known to have enjoyed spiritual authority and recognition. However, from the fourth century onwards, a patriarchal interpretation of theological tradition increasingly dominated, which excluded women from ministries and theological authority and denied their spiritual potential or reduced them to roles such as nuns and pious wives.

It was not until the modern era, increasingly from the Enlightenment onwards and especially in the 20th century, that a profound change in the understanding of the role of women began. Feminist movements and theological currents were increasingly committed to recognizing women as spiritual equals, intellectual equals and ethically competent. The introduction of women's suffrage, access to higher education and ultimately to theological faculties were important milestones on the road to greater equality. In the course of feminist theology, there was also a demand for critical reflection on patriarchal images of God and structures in the church.

Today, it is taken for granted - also from a democratic, human rights perspective - that women are just as worthy, educated and spiritually gifted as men. However, in many religious communities, including parts of the Catholic Church, there are still restrictions regarding the full equality and spiritual recognition of women. For this very reason, it remains important to understand the historical origins of these discriminations and to promote conscious, objective theological reflection in order to finally realize justice and equality without restrictions.

Today's image of women is essentially and naturally characterized by a clear awareness of equality, equal rights and social participation. Today, women claim their legal status as a matter of course, which is expressly enshrined in the German Basic Law ("*Men and women have equal rights*", Article 3 (2) of the Basic Law). This results in concrete expectations of social, professional and political equality, fair pay and equal career opportunities, regardless of gender or origin. *Female empowerment* is a central concept here, expressing the fact that women not only demand formal rights, but also want to exert an actual and active influence - both on decision-making processes and in social debates. Today, women expect to be heard and taken seriously on an equal footing, to contribute their perspectives, skills and experience and to actively shape social and political developments on an equal footing with men.

But apart from legends, there have always been influential women in the course of church history who worked *around the papal power* and sometimes had a significant influence on it - without holding the office themselves. In the 10th century, for example, the Roman noblewoman *Marozia* de facto dominated the Papal States and determined the appointment of several popes - decried by chroniclers as *a "pornocracy"*.

Marozia (c. 890-937) was an influential Roman noblewoman who exercised considerable influence over the papal office in the early 10th century. As the daughter of the noble family of the Theophylactes, she at times exercised considerable control over the occupation of the papal throne by using her political power and family connections. Her role went so far that several popes of her time were either directly or indirectly dependent on her, including her son, Pope John XI (931-935).

The term *"pornocracy"* (Greek: rule of prostitutes) was coined by later church historians in retrospect to portray this period (around 904 to 963) as morally corrupt and discredited by sexual debauchery and the nepotistic exercise of power. This negative assessment was primarily derived from the fact that women such as Marozia exercised great political influence in a patriarchal society and that they were accused of sexual and moral misconduct - in some cases with historical evidence, in others exaggerated by polemics.

The term is disreputable because it accuses women of abusing their power in strongly derogatory, sexualized language and at the same time condemns them morally. This view often concealed the actual political abilities and strategic skills of these women. From today's perspective, it can be seen as a positive effect that Marozia proved in an exemplary way how women could act politically effectively, even in a male-dominated society, although they were denied formal positions of power. To this day, her role encourages us to take a more differentiated historical view of female influence and to recognize that women had a significant impact on ecclesiastical and political developments even under difficult conditions.

However, these women were exceptions to the historical image of women, as they clearly contradicted the prevailing image of being and acting as women at the time - and therefore appear all the more remarkable.

Artistic evidence also testifies to the presence of women in the context of the office: for example, a 9th century mosaic in the Roman church of *Santa Prassede* shows the mother of Pope Paschal I with the title *"Episcopa Theodora"* (female form of bishop)

Historians suspect a special honor here: it is possible that close female relatives of high-ranking clerics were to be awarded such a title.

Some researchers, such as Dorothy Irvin, even believe that the mosaic could indicate an actual type of female "episcopate" - although this is disputed by the majority of (male) experts.

Overall, women have therefore been denied access to the ordained ministries (deacon, priest, bishop, pastor) throughout the history of the church. *Historically, the ordination of women can only be proven in the Montanist movement,* an early Christian prophetic group of the 2nd century, which was later condemned as heretical. The fact that Montanists regularly appointed women as priests contributed significantly to their condemnation as heretics at the time. Other fringe movements also showed some tendencies to give women liturgical roles, but in the church mainstream, women's ordination was consistently considered impossible. Until well into the 20th century, the view was widespread that men and women had different tasks due to their God-given differences - and the issue that the leadership of the church could also be a matter for women was not questioned.

It was not until the late 20th century that this view began to change, primarily due to the opening up of other Christian denominations and debates on reform within the church.

Today, however, women are claiming the full spiritual office and not just running alongside the Pope - and are demanding full equality in the church! They no longer want to exert only indirect influence and be analyzing, coordinating or communicating service staff and kitchen help, but want to take on equal and official responsibility and leadership positions. They want to become theological and social leaders and set the directives.

In the Catholic Church, however, popes have remained men to this day, and so far no real case has brought a woman anywhere near the papal office

For a long time, the Church was able to leave the pressing social, societal and legal question *"Is the papacy still exclusively male after a second female pope?"* unanswered by simply referring to its own tradition. But now these self-evident facts are beginning to falter. The social issue and reality of equal rights for all genders is becoming a theological one. A dialog is required.

# Biblical foundations: leadership and development of gender justice

If you look at the Bible, both supporters and opponents of women in church ministry can find arguments for their position. According to tradition, *Jesus Christ* himself appointed twelve men as his closest apostles (cf. Mt 10:1-4) - apparently no woman belonged to this circle. This fact is often interpreted as an expression of Jesus' will that the apostolic leadership office should remain male.

The authors of the New Testament also reflect the patriarchal culture of the time: *the First Letter to Timothy*, for example, contains the categorical instruction: *"I do not permit a woman to teach, nor to rule over a man; she must keep quiet"*. For centuries, such passages served as biblical legitimization for excluding women from preaching and leadership ministries.

At the same time, we find *evidence in* the Bible *of the involvement of women in* the early church. In his letters, *Paul* greets several women in leading roles. In Romans 16:7, for example, he calls a certain *Junia* *"famous among the apostles"* - which is understood by many exegetes as an indication that Junia herself was considered a female apostle.

In Romans 16:1-2, Paul recommends the *deaconess Phoebe* to the church in Rome and literally calls her *"diákonos"* (servant/deacon) of the church of Cenchrea. Even if it is disputed whether this word already refers to the church's ordained ministry, it is clear that women like Phoebe played an active role in ministry in the early church. *Women prophesied and prayed publicly* (cf. 1 Cor 11:5), and in the apostles' circle there were female disciples such as Mary Magdalene, who was referred to as the *"apostle of the apostles"* because she was the first to proclaim the message of the resurrection (John 20:18).

However, the *pastoral letters* also report disputes: *some women apparently acted as teachers in an effective and sustained manner*, which led to prohibitions.

The young churches therefore wrestled with the question of what role women were "allowed" to play in the assembly. For example, 1 Cor 14:34 warns: *"Women should keep silent in the assemblies"*, and 1 Tim 2 justifies the ban on teaching with the order of creation (Adam created first) and Eve's deception (cf. 1 Tim 2:13-14). Such texts reflect an *order of the time* that imposed *subordination* on women, *oppressed and discriminated against* them.

Nevertheless, there is also a *basic emancipatory tone* in the New Testament. Paul proclaims in Galatians 3:27-28 with regard to the baptismal equality of all believers: *"For all of you who were baptized into Christ have put on Christ. There is no longer Jew and Greek, slave and free, male and female, for you are all one in Christ Jesus"*. This theologically fundamental statement - *in Christ, social or gender difference no longer counts* - is often quoted by proponents of women's ordination. They argue: If in the church all the baptized have *"become Christ himself"* and have been given his identity without distinction, then *a new, ontologically defined difference in status between laity and clergy* should *not be established in this very community through ordination*.

In other words, an exclusive male clergy contradicts the message of unity and equality of baptism.

The Bible therefore does not offer a clear verdict that forever excludes women from church offices. Jesus himself gave no explicit instructions as to whether women were allowed to lead his church or not. The church of the first century knew of *female deacons and prophets*, but no female apostles or bishops *(episkopoi)*. Thus, the Holy Scriptures can be used to justify both a de facto *continuous male succession* of the apostles and the mandate to include all baptized persons, regardless of gender, in all ministries and offices of the church. The range of these biblical testimonies are still reflected in theological discourse today in such a way that they synchronize with today's social and legal self-image of equality.

## Voices of tradition on women in office

In the first Christian centuries and in the Middle Ages, an overwhelming majority of male voices in theology and church leadership emerged against women in the sacramental ministry. Church fathers such as Tertullian, Origen, Epiphanius of Salamis and St. Augustine formulated clear rejections. *Tertullian* (ca. 200 AD), for example, wrote a clear polemic against communities that allowed women to perform liturgical functions: *"A woman is not permitted to speak in the church, nor to teach ... and to exercise no office reserved for men, and certainly no priestly office"*. The church father *Epiphanius* was outraged by a group in Arabia that allowed women to celebrate the Eucharist, calling it *"ungodly, sacrilegious and devilish"*. He emphasized: *"From the Lord there is the office of deaconess, but not to be a priestess... Never was a woman called to these [offices]. For although there were, for example, the four daughters of Philip who spoke prophetically, they were not priestesses"*.

Epiphanius even argued with the prominent position *of Mary:* if God had ever intended a woman to be a priest, he would have given it to Mary, the mother of Jesus - *"but he did not think this was good"*.

This logic - Mary, as the highest of all creatures of the female sex, had no priestly ministry - was intended to demonstrate that priesthood was inherently male. But it was just an argument pulled out of thin air in order not to open the door even a little with this argument.

Councils of the early church also confirmed this exclusion. The *Council of Laodicea* (around 360), for example, stated succinctly: *"The so-called presbyteresses or overseers may not be ordained in the church"*. The early Christian church order *Didascalia Apostolorum* (3rd century) explains that although Jesus had female disciples, *"if it had been necessary for women to teach, our teacher would have appointed them to preach with us [apostles]"*.

Such statements second and thus cement the conviction that Christ himself reserved the ministries exclusively for men.

In *the Middle Ages*, this view continued in sometimes drastic judgments. St. *Thomas Aquinas* (1225-1274), one of the greatest teachers of the Church, wrote that women were created in the image of God just like men and had the same basic dignity. Nevertheless, he considered women to be subordinate to men and, following Aristotle, judged them to be *"something deficient and unsuccessful"* in the order of creation.

Thomas strictly rejected a teaching or leadership position, because *"teaching and public ministry in the church were a matter for superiors and not for subordinates, to whom women essentially belonged due to their gender"*. He also believed that women lacked the necessary spiritual wisdom for such offices and that preaching women could *"seduce men into lust"*.

As harsh as these three traditional views seem today, for centuries they were representative of patriarchal church theology. Many theologians considered women to be naturally subordinate to men and therefore unsuitable to exercise sacred leadership.

## Voices of today's modern age on women in office

The debate on the admission of women to ordained ministries in the Catholic Church has gained considerable and lasting intensity since the last century. Numerous voices from the Church and society are calling for an urgent change in this practice.

One well-known example is the former German ambassador to the Holy See, Annette Schavan. The political conservative emphasizes the need to continue the debate on the ordination of women.

There is also movement within the bishops' conferences. Some bishops are becoming more open to discussions about the role of women in the church and are questioning traditional positions. For example, the chairman of the German Bishops' Conference, Bishop Georg Bätzing, has stated that he does not consider the issue of women's ordination to be closed and that a decision will have to be made soon.

Many believers and theologians are also in favor of opening up ordained ministries to women. They argue that by including women in all ministries, the church will not only do justice to its message of equality and justice, but must also gain relevance and credibility in modern society.

In addition, it should not be overlooked that women are and were highly recognized in monastic and charitable contexts. Abbesses led convents, mystics such as *Hildegard von Bingen* had spiritual influence (even if not official authority). *Female saints* and teachers of the faith were venerated - so that modernity can no longer draw a clear line in the ordained ministry. The assessment that women should now be included at the altar and ambo is therefore inevitably linked to the appreciation of their person - and to a role model that is now firmly established and equal. In the modern age, the Church has reflected on its own image of women and in many cases affirmed it positively - i.e. confirmed that a decision in favor of equal rights in the ordained ministry is to be pronounced.

An initial look at the course of time to date shows that the voices of the Church Fathers and Doctors of the Church were unanimous in their rejection of women in church leadership. They based this on biblical interpretations, on the historically evolved tradition of apostolic succession and on the idea of a God-given gender order in which women were subject to men.

Today, new theological insights, social developments and statuses as well as changing expectations form an essential and weighty foundation for the Church's magisterium to enable the practice of the priesthood for women and to speak out clearly for gender equality. Today, the gender-neutral nature of the priesthood is and must be upheld - instead of an outdated male bonding. The old men's adherence to the male bonds only delays the debate on the decision for gender justice by a few years, as younger men are socialized quite differently today.

They are asked why they recognize the Basic Law, which considers women and men to have equal rights - all other views are considered unjust and discriminatory in society - and are therefore rejected as discreditable.

# Women in ordained ministries - status of Catholic canon law

The current Catholic legal situation enshrines tradition: according to the 1983 Code of Canon Law (CIC), *"only a baptized man* can *validly receive holy orders"* (Canon 1024). In other words, every ordained office - deacon, priest or bishop - is restricted to men. According to current law, a woman can therefore neither become a priest nor, consequently, a bishop or pope.

This prohibition is strictly enforced by canonical sanctions. The attempt to ordain a woman results in automatic excommunication. As early as 2007, the Congregation for the Doctrine of the Faith made it clear that all those involved in a so-called "ordination of women" exclude themselves from the sacraments. In 2021, this penalty was even expressly included in canon law (Canon 1379 §3 CIC). The Church thus treats the ordination of a woman as a serious offense by men against unity and the sacramental order.

At the same time, the Church's highest magisterium has repeatedly emphasized that this is not merely a law, but an immutable teaching. The 1976 declaration *Inter insigniores* of the Congregation for the Doctrine of the Faith states unequivocally: *"The Catholic Church has never held the view that women can be validly ordained as priests or bishops."* In his 1994 Apostolic Exhortation *Ordinatio Sacerdotalis*, Pope John Paul II formulated the claim to decide this question once and for all. In paragraph 4 he solemnly declared: *"...that the Church has no authority to confer priestly ordination on women and that all the faithful of the Church must definitively abide by this decision".* By faithful, both men and women are meant. But haven't men made a calculation without the host when deciding on women?

The Congregation for the Doctrine of the Faith even specified a year later that this was to be understood as a *"definitive teaching"* - *in* the opinion of many, therefore, *infallible* or at least irreformable.

This is comparable to ordering a car, where certain equipment features are only available in a mandatory combination with other equipment features: the seat heating is only available if the light package is also booked. This is called a *mandatory combination*.

So anyone who wants to introduce the ordination of women must recognize that the Pope is infallible - or at least that partial refomability can exist while infallibility continues to exist? Only in this way can the Catholic Church escape its straitjacket of the bound combination.

In the last century, any discussion about women in the priesthood was effectively stopped within the Catholic Church - even though the theological dialog and discourse on the subject was not broken off. This also proves the Pope's error in controlling silent mouths on this topic.

Nevertheless, the Vatican still emphasizes today that this "no" is binding and not a mere disciplinary rule, but is based on the divine order of the Church.

However, there are also contradictory signals, indications and visions of a different future not only in the discourse - but also in the church's doctrinal structure: interestingly, in the encyclical *Pacem in terris* (as early as 1963), Pope *John XXIII* recognized the *equal rights of men and women* with regard to career choices - and explicitly also in relation to spiritual professions. Under the heading *"Right to free choice of the state of life"*, he writes: *"Moreover, men have the inviolable right to choose the state of life they deem good, that is, either to found a family (...) or to enter the priesthood or the religious order"* (Pacem in terris, no. 9).

*John XXIII explicitly grants women the right to choose and exercise the priesthood.* He justifies this with the *"sign of the times"* - i.e. a whole century ago - that women should participate in public life and demand rights in accordance with their dignity. This passage seems surprisingly progressive today - even if his successors did not repeat it.

If this encyclical statement by the pope of the time is also infallible, then it does not need to be repeated and thus it is 1:1 in the infallibility of different popes - one in favor of the ordination of women, the other against the ordination of women. This contradiction also seems to cancel out the logic of infallibility, so that it does not exist and then one of the two variants would have to apply - possibly the one that is more up-to-date and synchronized with social realities, i.e. the more modern statement.

In fact, the *status quo* as well as a formulated *vision* with a mandate for adaptation thus remains clear: according to Catholic law, there can currently be no female priests and consequently no female popes. Only after an adaptation and reformation of the law in the sense of equal rights enshrined in the constitution can there be female priests and consequently a female pope in the near future.

The Church of Rome still insists that there does not seem to be any need or authority for change in this area.

Once again, it is a forced combination that is intended to substantiate this view. A two-component glue: it is both about a canon law that can be changed by a corresponding authority, but cannot be changed due to the dependencies in the Vatican - and it is about a supposedly divine law in the sense of the interpretation of the environment of Jesus Christ, which no one else is able to interpret.

The subjectivity of interpretations and their social embedding make the debate about this "two-component glue", about the so-called reformable infallibility of the Pope, particularly exciting

At the heart of this is the question of whether a pope will succeed in convincing those around him and the community of officials in Rome of his decision to ordain women. Or vice versa: Could a younger, more open-minded environment in the Vatican with more modern views on equal rights accompany and convince a possibly older and more conservative pope in such a way that a joint decision on gender equality and the availability of all church ministries for women can be made in a timely manner?

If a joint decision in favor of women's ordination cannot be reached, it is conceivable that a progressive pope alone could or must make this decision on gender equality in church ministries.

However, there is also a third possible path that could be dictated by social changes: Declining membership numbers among believers and church ministers and employees, especially if modern and committed women turn away from the church in disappointment, or if social movements such as *Maria 2.0* or *We Are Church* significantly increase the pressure for equal rights, the church could ultimately be moved to make a decision on equal rights in the priesthood. Because equality and human rights are not false dogmas, but meaningful and necessary goals and structures in life and therefore also appropriate for a vibrant and people-friendly church.

The ordination of women alone would mean that women could in principle be ordained as priests, bishops or other ecclesiastical offices. If full gender equality in ordination were implemented in the Catholic Church, it would theoretically also be possible to elect a woman as Pope.

However, the election of a female pope presupposes that not only ordination is opened up to women, but also that the legal and theological conditions are created for a woman to be elected to the highest office of the Catholic Church. This would require changes to canon law and church doctrine.

Historically and currently, such a development has not yet been implemented or planned in the Catholic Church. However, discussions about a possible "female pope" do exist in the context of the theological dialogs about gender justice and equality within the church.

In order for a woman to be effectively elected to the highest office in the Roman Catholic Church, i.e. as Pope, both legal and theological prerequisites must be changed or created, actually simply as follows:

**Legal requirements in canon law**

- **Change in canon law (CIC):**
  According to current canon law (Codex Iuris Canonici, Canon 1024), ordination to the priesthood is reserved exclusively for men.

*CIC, can. 1024: "Holy Orders are validly received only by a baptized man."*

This canon would have to be explicitly amended or repealed in order to allow women to be ordained as priests and later as bishops. Without this change, no woman is eligible for higher ecclesiastical offices.

- **Change to the right of election to the papal office:**
  The current apostolic constitution on the election of popes (currently: *Universi Dominici Gregis*) stipulates that only male cardinals (i.e. ordained bishops or priests) may elect and be elected pope. This regulation would have to be adapted so that women could be formally appointed as cardinals and elected accordingly.

**Theological prerequisites**

- **Revision of Catholic doctrine on the understanding of sacramental ministry:**
  Catholic theology justifies the exclusion of women on the basis of tradition (referring to Jesus, who probably only appointed male apostles) and the interpretation that the priest must represent Christ as a man ("in persona Christi"). A theological reassessment would have to take place in order to make the admission of women as priests and bishops compatible with the understanding of priesthood and sacramentality.

- **Re-interpretation of tradition and Scripture:**
  The historical restriction to men is often justified with reference to the apostles (all male). For a female pope, biblical texts and tradition would have to be reinterpreted in order to demonstrate that gender exclusivity is not an immutable divine commandment, but is culturally determined.

- **Theological re-evaluation of the papal office:** The theological and dogmatic definition of the papal office would have to be formulated in a gender-neutral way or explicitly opened up to women. This would involve clarifying how female office holders could represent the role of the "Vicar of Christ" (Vicarius Christi).

A female pope would therefore not be possible through political or structural changes alone. What is needed is a fundamental legal and theological reorientation of the Catholic Church, its ministerial structures and its self-image in the above-mentioned, few and actually simple points. Such adjustments would be effective, sustainable and would have to be decided, proclaimed and implemented at the highest level (church council or papal decision with a global impact).

## Recent theological arguments for equal rights in the ministry

Numerous *theologians and believers* have made weighty arguments in favor of granting women access to all church ministries, including the priesthood and papacy. These arguments emphasize justice, fidelity to the Bible and the vitality of tradition:

- *A new reading of biblical findings:* Proponents such as biblical scholar Marie-Theres Wacker *point out that the historical evidence in the New Testament is by no means as clearly against women in ministry* as is often claimed. On the contrary, there are *"some good arguments for the ordination of women"* in the Bible.

In addition to the women already mentioned, such as *Junia* or *Phoebe*, they point out that Jesus *did not make any statement* that excludes women from any kind of ministry. *The narrow interpretation that Jesus' choice of the twelve means a ban for all time is addressed as exegetically dubious.* Theologian *Claudia Lücking-Michel* notes that *all church arguments can "not only be refuted, but virtually picked apart"*, especially the *"inaccurate assertion that the exclusion of women is Christ's will".* This interpretation is evidence of a *superficial approach to*

*Jesus' work* - nowhere does it contain any reference to *never* ordaining women.

Rather, Jesus overcame traditional barriers through his interaction with women (such as the Samaritan woman, John 4, or Mary Magdalene).

- *Theology of baptism and equality in Christ:* As mentioned above, Galatians 3:28 - *"not male and female, for you are all one in Christ"* - is seen as a central principle. From this follows a strong *principle of equality* within the church. *"The baptized have become Christ himself... no longer differ from one another,"* emphasizes Marlis Gielen, referring to the old baptismal tradition.

If baptism makes everyone fundamentally equal, then *ordination cannot create a new difference in status.*

This argument goes to the heart of the sacramental hierarchy: why an exclusive caste of priests (and a male one at that) if all believers are "a nation of priests" (cf. 1 Peter 2:9)? Proponents emphasize the *universal vocation of all the baptized.* They argue that the *ordained ministry should be service and not domination* - and women are just as called to serve the Word and Sacrament as men.

- *Church prohibition of discrimination:* In *Gaudium et Spes* 29, the *Second Vatican Council* stated unequivocally: *"All forms of discrimination... on the basis of sex have been overcome and must be eradicated, since they are contrary to God's plan".* According to the Central Committee of German Catholics (ZdK), this *divine prohibition of discrimination places the burden of justification* on the Church as to why it nevertheless treats people unequally.

*It is not the access of women to the ministry that must be justified, but their exclusion,* the German Catholics stated in the "Osnabrück Theses" in 2017. Proponents see no viable justification for this unequal treatment. For Sister Katharina Ganz, Superior of the Oberzell Franciscan Sisters, it is *"no longer acceptable in our culture that the door to ordained ministries remains closed to women".* She speaks of a *"painful justice gap"* in the church. An unjust law has no validity - *lex iniusta non obligat*, argue some canon lawyers who defend the illegal ordination of women.

- *Development of doctrine and tradition:* Throughout history, the Church has often changed its practice as new understandings have matured. *Pope Pius XII* emphasized in 1947: *"Everyone knows that the Church can change and abolish* what *it has established."*

Why shouldn't the same apply here? Opponents of an opening claim that the No is *infallible*. But even high-ranking churchmen cast doubt on this: Cardinal *Jean-Claude Hollerich* said in 2023 that it was *"probably not an infallible doctrine"* and that *"with time"* a pope could decide differently. Pope *Francis* himself recently emphasized that *"the last word [on this issue] has not yet been spoken"*. Supporters also point out that *many of today's doctrinal statements by previous popes were revised* as soon as findings changed - be it on religious freedom, marriage or science. *Tradition is alive*, not static. What is considered unchangeable today can be seen in a new light tomorrow, just as councils have done in the past.

- *Charisms and vocations:* In practice, many feel that women *feel called* by God *to serve at the altar.* Systematically rejecting these vocations seems theologically problematic. As early as *1976, the Pontifical Biblical Commission* established that *nothing in the Bible clearly speaks against the ordination of women.*

But if God gives charisms, why should the church suppress them? *Women have long proven* that they can preach, lead and provide pastoral care (e.g. as theologians, pastoral workers, church leaders). As Anglican theologian *Dr. Jane Morris* put it: *"If God endows a woman with the gifts of a priest, who are we to deny it?"* It is emphasized that the *Holy Spirit can also take women into ministry* - especially since Pentecost fulfilled everyone, *"sons and daughters shall prophesy"* (Joel 3:1).

The sum of these arguments leads to the conviction of many Catholic believers: *The exclusion of women from ordained ministries lacks a convincing theological justification and damages the credibility of the Church.* Rather, it contradicts the spirit of Jesus, who emphasized the dignity of all people - regardless of gender. Instead, it is time to *fully recognize* the gifts and callings of women. The church would not become poorer, but richer through women in ministry. Last but not least, they point to the practical level: *in many churches today, women bear the main burden of preaching and church leadership*, while priests are in short supply. Opening up the ministries would therefore also be a response to pastoral and organizational needs.

# Developments in other Christian denominations

A look beyond the Catholic horizon shows that other churches *have indeed appointed women to the highest spiritual offices* in recent decades. These experiences are being closely observed in the debate within the Catholic Church.

*Anglican churches:* In parts of the *Anglican Communion* (Church of England, Episcopal Church USA and others), women began to be admitted to the priesthood as early as the 1970s. The *Episcopal Church in the USA* ordained its first female priests in 1976, followed by the *Anglican Church of New Zealand* in 1977. Historically significant was the consecration of *Barbara Clementine Harris* as an Anglican *bishop* in 1989 (suffragan bishop in Massachusetts, USA - the first female bishop in the Anglican Communion). In 1990, *Penny Jamieson* became the first woman diocesan bishop (leading bishop of a diocese) in New Zealand. In the *Church of England* itself, women have been admitted to the priesthood since 1994 and to the episcopate since 2014. In 2015, *Libby Lane* became the first female bishop in the Church of England, followed by *Rachel Treweek* as the first female diocesan bishop. There are now female bishops in almost all Anglican provinces; in 2006, *Katharine Jefferts Schori* became the first woman to be elected Primate (leading archbishop) of an Anglican church - she headed the Episcopal Church USA until 2015.

Anglicans have thus shown that *women can indeed hold the highest offices of leadership - comparable to the Pope*. Interestingly, large parts of the Anglican world church today accept women in the office of bishop as regular and normal.

*Protestant churches:* In the Protestant churches (Lutheran, Reformed, Methodist and others), the *ordination of women is now widespread*. The first pioneers were women in free churches as early as the 19th century. In the large regional churches, the opening up usually began after the Second World War: e.g. in 1948 in the Protestant Church in Hesse-Nassau the first ordained female pastor. In the *Lutheran churches of Scandinavia*, women were given access to all ministries from the 1960s onwards. *Women bishops* are now a matter of course in many Protestant churches; *Margot Käßmann*, for example, is widely known as the former chair of the EKD Council (2009-2010), and in *Switzerland, Kathrin Bold-Wendebourg* and *Sabine Brunner* are also women church leaders.

*Old Catholic Church:* The case of the *Old Catholic Churches* (Union of Utrecht), which are separate from Rome, is interesting. In these churches, which are traditionally very Catholic, women have been admitted to ordained ministries since the 1980s. In 1982, the International Bishops' Conference allowed the member churches to ordain women to the diaconate. From 1987, such ordinations took place in the Old Catholic Church in Switzerland and Germany.

In 1989, the German Old Catholic Synod spoke out *in favor of admitting women to the priesthood*.

*Priests* are now also active *in* some Old Catholic churches - for example in Austria and the Netherlands. This shows that a Catholic church has integrated the ordination of women without giving up its claim to catholicity.

All in all, these examples show that Christianity is divided on the issue, and many communities have had good experiences with women in top spiritual positions. It is often emphasized that *spiritual gifts are not bound to one gender* - preaching, pastoral care and leadership are just as successful for women as for men. *The Catholic Church is isolated here* with its absolute ban

The examples of other denominations are encouraging: they prove that *a female bishop or even a female head of church (equivalent to the pope)* is possible without breaking up the church. *A woman at the altar or in the bishop's chair is a* reality in many churches today - so why not in Rome in the office of a female pope?

# Looking to the present and the future: Synodal processes, initiatives and theologians - and the realization of a female pope

In recent years, the debate about women in church ministry has gained considerable momentum within the Catholic Church. *Numerous initiatives and reform movements* are pushing for change, while *high-ranking church representatives* also making differentiated statements.

In Germany in particular, the *Synodal Path* (2019-2023) caused a stir. This reform forum of bishops and laypeople explicitly addressed the topic of women in ministries and offices. In September 2022 , the Synodal Assembly voted overwhelmingly (92% of participants, including 82% of bishops) in favor of a resolution that expects the Vatican *to adapt the teaching of Ordinatio Sacerdotalis (1994).*

The text of the resolution states: *"The doctrine of 'Ordinatio Sacerdotalis' is widely not accepted and not understood by the people of God. Therefore, the question must be addressed to the highest authority in the Church (Pope and Council) as to whether this teaching does not need to be examined... Whether the teaching is infallibly binding or not must be clarified."*

In other words, *a large majority of even the German bishops consider the women's issue to be worthy of change* and not closed.

The Chairman of the German Bishops' Conference, Bishop Georg Bätzing, said in 2020: *"For me, the issue is not closed, but it is an open question in the Church and must be treated as such"*. In a society that sees equality as a fundamental right, he could not see *"how the demand for ordained ministries for women could be an aberration"*.

Countless *initiatives* are active *at grassroots level*. In Germany, the *Maria 2.0* movement caused a sensation in 2019: women organized a "church strike" and loudly demanded *access for women to all ministries, including the priesthood*. The *Catholic Women's Community of Germany (kfd)* has been calling for "all ministries and offices" for women since the 1990s.

These movements make it clear that *far beyond academic circles*, Catholic women (and men too) see the issue as an urgent one.

Some also ask with pressure: *What image of God does* a church convey that labels women as unworthy of a leadership role? Is it not giving a sign that the "supreme representative of Christ" must of course be a man - and thus feeding the idea of a *predominantly male image of God*?

Feminist theologians such as *Elisabeth Schüssler Fiorenza* criticize the fact that a male-dominated ministry *"cements patriarchal structures that push women into subordinate roles"*. She calls for a return to the "original dynamics" of the early churches, in which women played an active role. A church that systematically excludes women from leadership, according to Fiorenza, *misses a core mission of the Gospel*, namely to realize justice and participation for all.

*The credibility* of the church is also at stake. Many believers - especially young women - can no longer reconcile the unequal treatment with their conscience and leave the church. They ask beforehand: How can the church call for *human rights and equality in society and politics*, but treat women as secondary in its own house?

In view of the growing dissatisfaction with the status quo, many are asking themselves: *what could change look like in practice?* One way often mentioned is a *worldwide synodal consultation process* or even a *Vatican Council* to discuss the issue at the highest level. This is what the German Synodal Way proposed - to address the question to the Pope and the Council.

Although the office of pope in the Catholic Church is currently only held by men, the issue has long been on the table and has stirred up emotions from the grassroots to the hierarchy.

Historically, there has never been a female pope - except in legends - but the future is open. Perhaps we will actually see a *woman in the Chair of Peter* in the near future, or perhaps it will remain an unfulfilled dream of many. One thing is certain: the discussion about women in church leadership positions will continue, driven by the spirit of justice and the hope for a renewed church. *Shaping the papacy for all genders will be a decision on how seriously the Church takes its own message of the equality of all in Christ.*

# Chapter 2:
# Was Jesus queer - and what does that say about our images of God?

*The chapter deals with the theological question of whether Jesus of Nazareth was queer and what impact such a perspective has on our images of God today. Queer theology argues that Jesus consciously transgressed social norms regarding gender and sexuality, for example through his close emotional bond with the so-called "beloved disciple" or by healing the servant of a Roman centurion, which some interpret as an encounter with a same-sex partnership. Jesus' unmarried status and his unconventional statements about family also leave room for interpretations beyond traditional heteronormative role models. Queer theologians such as Marcella Althaus-Reid and Patrick S. Cheng see Jesus as an embodiment of love that transcends boundaries, breaking down traditional categories and promoting theological inclusivity. In contrast, conservative voices argue that such interpretations are speculative and distort the message of Jesus. Nevertheless, a queer Christology offers opportunities for greater identification, inclusion and liberation of marginalized groups within the church.*

- **Question:** *How does our understanding of Jesus Christ and God's love change when we consciously think of Jesus beyond traditional gender and sexuality norms, and what consequences does this have for the church and society?*
- **Question:** *Is a church that insists on a Jesus who must have lived a strictly heteronormative life not rather an expression of its own fears and prejudices that betray the universal message of Jesus' boundless love?*
- **Option for action:** *The Catholic Church should openly acknowledge that traditional heteronormative ideas about Jesus and God are only one of many possible interpretations, and actively create theological spaces in which queer perspectives on Jesus can be respectfully discussed and integrated.*

- **Training option:** Clergy, believers and students in religious education should develop skills in queer theological hermeneutics as well as intercultural and gender-sensitive pedagogy, for example through seminars that analyze biblical texts from a queer perspective and encourage participants to reflexively question social norms in order to live an authentic and inclusive faith practice in a credible way.

The topic *"Was Jesus queer?"* may seem unusual at first glance. However, there is a serious theological interest behind it: What do Jesus' lifestyle and relationships say about his humanity and about God's nature? In theology and the church, some authors are increasingly discussing whether Jesus of Nazareth thought and lived in any way *queer* - i.e. outside of strict heteronormative categories - and what consequences such a perspective would have for our image of God today.

Queer theologians emphasize that Jesus broke through social gender norms and behaved unusually. At the same time, conservative voices warn against speculating about Jesus' sexuality and his emotional and therefore possibly also sexual orientation. In the following, we shed light on biblical references, queer theological interpretations, cultural perspectives and possible implications of a *queer Christology* - understandable for all, yet theologically sound.

# Biblical references: Emotionality, physicality and sexuality of Jesus

The Gospels portray Jesus as a person with deep emotions and physical affection.

*Emotionality:* Jesus weeps at the grave of his friend Lazarus (John 11:35) and shows affection for his disciples. The Gospel of John tells us that a disciple *"whom Jesus loved"* lay on Jesus' chest during the Last Supper (John 13:23) - a gesture of intimate closeness. The Gospel of Mark also enigmatically reports of an *"unknown young man"* who follows Jesus to Gethsemane and then flees naked (Mark 14:51-52).

*Physicality:* Jesus did not shy away from physical closeness - he embraced children, washed his disciples' feet and allowed the *"beloved disciple"* to rest by his side.

Such scenes show Jesus as a *physically devoted* man who did not bring tenderness and service into conflict with his masculinity (cf. John 13).

*Sexuality:* It is striking that the Bible does not ascribe a heteronormative relationship to Jesus. Contrary to what was customary for Jewish rabbis, nowhere is a wife or romantic partner of Jesus mentioned. Jesus even spoke positively about people who abstain from marriage: *"There are those who have been born of the womb... and have cut themselves off for the sake of the kingdom of heaven"* (Mt 19:12) - a word that some understand as early recognition of people who do not fit into the usual marriage and family model. Jesus' miracle for the *Roman centurion* is just as significant: he asks Jesus to heal his sick *pais* (Greek: "boy/servant"). Some exegetes - including the theologian Bob Shore-Goss - interpret the *pais* as the centurion's young lover and thus the miracle as Jesus' encounter with a same-sex couple. In fact, Jesus praises the faith of this centurion in the highest terms and finds *"no greater faith in all Israel"* (Mt 8:10) - without any word of rebuke for the relationship.

To this day, millions of Christians repeat the humble words of the centurion at Mass: *"Lord, I am not worthy that you should enter under my roof..."* - often without realizing that, according to Shore-Goss, these words came from the mouth of a man in a homoerotic relationship. The Bible does *not* provide *a direct account* of a sexual relationship with Jesus. However, *indirect references* - close male friendships, unconventional family statements (cf. Mk 3:35) and the appreciation of *"eunuchs"* - leave room for interpretations beyond one-dimensional role models.

Queer theologians ask: *Is it a coincidence that the favorite disciple and Lazarus are referred to as "those whom Jesus loved"?*

## Queer theological interpretations of Jesus' life

Queer theologians have developed a variety of interpretations based on such biblical passages. They see Jesus as someone who radically questioned social norms of gender and sexuality. The Argentinian pioneer of queer theology *Marcella Althaus-Reid*, for example, writes about a *"queer God"*: God's nature cannot be understood within the narrow boundaries of heteronormativity and purity laws. Specifically, she transfers this to Jesus, the incarnate second person of the Trinity. Althaus-Reid plays with erotic imagery: *"We could say that the Son lies with his Magdalene and his Lazarus,"* she imagines - Jesus thus connected in love with a woman *and* a man at the same time. This consciousness-expanding idea of a *quasi-polyamorous* Jesus pursues a theological goal: it is intended to break up the *"illusory uniqueness"* of the one permitted model of love - Althaus-Reid speaks of the *"death of the monogamous lover"*. God is *"not a monogamous patriarch, but God's love is exuberant, diverse and disordered"*.

As long as God is fixed in a white-male-heterosexual image, women, queers and the poor will remain excluded. Only a *"queer God"*, who is present in the loving community of outcasts, makes true liberation possible. Althaus-Reid therefore calls on female theologians to shed their false shame - *"to take off their pious underwear"* - and to incorporate physicality and their own sexuality into theology. This *"indecent theology"* understandably came up against the need for integration: Conservatives accused her of *perverting* Christianity and desecrating the holiness of Jesus. Progressive voices, on the other hand, celebrated Althaus-Reid as a courageous thinker who sought God's presence precisely among the previously "indecent" excluded.

Other queer theologians also provide inspiring impulses. Some of them are explained below:

In *Radical Love* (2011), *Patrick S. Cheng* emphasizes the incarnation *of radical love: "God is the very manifestation of a love that is so extreme that it dissolves existing boundaries"*, he writes - in other words, God manifests a love that is so extreme that it dissolves existing boundaries. Cheng therefore sees Christ as the *incarnation of this boundary-crossing love*: in Jesus, God transcends all sexuality and gender boundaries. In the *"Queer Christ"* chapter of his book, Cheng explains that Jesus transcends all restrictive norms through his love and suffering and thus becomes the *archetype of* God's *queering* (i.e. liberating, alienating) power.

Cheng and Althaus-Reid see Jesus' passion in particular - being flogged and mocked - as a form of *identification with queers:* Jesus does not fit into the patriarchal ideal of masculinity and is exposed, degraded and violated, just as many queer people experience discrimination. Yet it is precisely in this vulnerability and his *radical understanding of love* that a divine solidarity with the outcasts lies.

Catholic theologian *James Alison*, himself a gay man, makes a similar argument: at its core, Christianity embodies *unconditional love and liberation for all people*. For Alison, traditional church teachings that condemn same-sex lovers are based more on social prejudice than on Jesus' message. Any discrimination - including against LGBTQIA+ people - denies the basic message of the Gospel. Alison speaks of modern scapegoats: queer people are unjustly made scapegoats in the church structure, although they *"do nothing but live their lives" - in the spirit of Jesus Christ*. By excluding them, the church betrays its own message of love and redemption. His conclusion: Christian doctrine does not have to be interpreted in a heteronormative way, but on the contrary contains a radical openness for all. Alison pleads for a *relaxed and non-blaming* approach to the topic - after all, from a Christian perspective, being queer is not a stigma, but part of the diversity God intended.

Finally, New Testament scholar *Tat-siong Benny Liew* has interpreted the Gospel of John *queerly* from an Asian-American perspective. In a much-discussed essay (2009), Liew reads certain scenes as conscious *queer codes:* Jesus' humble washing of the disciples' feet and the intimate situation of the favorite disciple leaning on Jesus' breast at the Last Supper, for example, he interprets as a deliberate *softening of gender roles*. Jesus takes on the role of a servant when washing feet - an act that was often reserved for women or slaves in Jesus' time - and thus breaks through the male hierarchy. According to Liew, the intimate breast situation with John could be a subtle signal of a non-heteronormative familiarity.

Liew's theories even went so far as to describe Jesus as a kind of *"drag king"* with queer desires. This sparked dialog in the USA: in 2018, conservatives called for Liew to be dismissed from his Catholic university. Such heated debates show how contested the terrain of a queer interpretation of Jesus was at the time. Nevertheless, Liew and other innovative exegetes are continuing the conversation: they are asking whether trans or non-binary people can also find their identity in Christ.

Some theologians now think of the person of Christ as an *"inclusive space"* that transcends traditional gender categories. After all, even in mysticism there were alternatives to the purely male view of Christ - such as depictions of Christ as maternal or androgynous.

Queer theology picks up on these threads and develops an image of Christ as a *universal, cross-gender liberator figure.*

## Cultural and psychological perspectives

In addition to biblical and theological findings, it is worth taking a look at the *cultural and social context* of Jesus' life - and how our own perspective colors our perception. Terms such as "gay", "queer" or "sexual orientation" did not exist in antiquity. At the time, same-sex acts were primarily understood as a *violation of gender roles*: The Torah states that if a man lies with a man as with a woman, it is *"an abomination"* (Lev 18:22). This was based on the ancient idea that a man would lose his masculine honor by taking on a passive role - he would *"feminize"* himself and submit, which was considered a disgrace at the time.

Today, it's not just about gender, about the difference between female and male, but also about sexual orientation.

Homosexuality was therefore not a sign of identity at the time, but an extreme case of role reversal. At the same time, *homoerotic relationships* were by no means unknown - especially in the Greco-Roman environment, for example, relationships (between older and younger men) were considered common. Jesus himself was active in Galilee and Judea, where strict Jewish sexual morals prevailed, but where Hellenistic influence was also noticeable. He never directly addressed the topic of homosexuality. However, his interaction with people often broke cultural taboos: he allowed women such as Mary of Bethany to speak and anoint him, which caused offense at the time; he talked alone with a Samaritan woman at the well; and he traveled through the country with a wandering *circle of friends* of men and women - an unconventional lifestyle beyond the traditional nuclear family.

*Intimacy and closeness with men:* In many Middle Eastern cultures, physical closeness between men (hugging, lying next to each other while eating) is more normal than in the modern West. According to Jewish custom, the Last Supper took place in a reclining position, side by side - the fact that John was leaning so close to Jesus did not necessarily mean anything sexual to those present. At the same time, it is remarkable *who* the Gospel of John explicitly emphasizes as *"the disciple whom Jesus loved"* - there was obviously a special emotional bond. From a psychological point of view, people (including spiritual leaders) look for confidants, and Jesus probably had his preferred companions in his inner circle (Peter, James, John - and perhaps John as his "favorite disciple"). The question arises as to why the tradition emphasizes this special love. Some interpreters, such as Theodore Jennings Jr., believe that the Gospel of John deliberately *idealizes* a close male friendship here and gives it homoerotic traits. Others simply see it as emphasizing *the love of friends* (Greek *philia*). One thing is certain: Jesus cultivated *intimate fellowship* with men, without shying away from leaning on, touching or emotional connection - something that was unusual in the macho cultures of his (and our) time. He thus demonstrated a *different masculinity* that was allowed to be tender and vulnerable. The social scientist *Halvor Moxnes* describes Jesus as a man who shattered traditional role models and established a new, inclusive community.

*Social gender roles:* Contrary to social expectations, Jesus lived in an *unattached status*. In Jewish eyes, the unmarried, childless man was actually considered an exception - *"Be fruitful and multiply"* (Genesis 1:28) was the norm. The fact that Jesus went about at the age of 30+, unmarried, could be seen as unusual. Some may have suspected a special calling (similar to the Ezekiel desert ascetics) behind it. In fact, Jesus emphasized a *new kind of family*: "Whoever does the will of God is brother, sister and mother to me" (Mk 3:35) - in other words, he defined the spiritual bond through blood ties. In doing so, he relativized the heteronormative nuclear family in favour of a *chosen family* of disciples. It was also culturally revolutionary that Jesus integrated women into his circle (Luke 8:1-3) and gave them important roles (witnesses of the resurrection). He transcended strictly separate spheres of *"male public"* and *"female private"*. Some queer thinkers, such as *Virginia Mollenkott*, go in speculative directions: Mollenkott asked whether Jesus could not be thought of as *intersexual* in a sense - he was, after all, conceived without a biological father, which transcends the boundaries of male/female. This may seem like daring theopoetics, but it shows the desire to explore *Jesus' identity beyond binary gender categories*.

*Psychological aspects:* How we see Jesus often says a lot about ourselves. An anecdote by the theologian *Shore-Goss* illustrates this: A lesbian student had said to him, *"Jesus wasn't gay, he was perfect"*. Behind this is the idea that *queer* is something (in)pure or (in)perfect - a deeply internalized (pre)judgment. But if Jesus - the *perfect* man and without sin - could theoretically have been gay or queer, what would that say about queer people? Shore-Goss puts it pointedly: If Jesus was perfect and gay, *"only homosexuals actually go to heaven"* - a possibly ironic, but possibly logical point.

This train of thought is intended as a wake-up call. It shows the extent to which traditional ideas of holiness have been linked to heteronormative assumptions. Psychologically, the idea of a *queer Jesus* can be relieving and empowering: For LGBTQIA+ Christians, Jesus could finally be someone who shares and fully accepts their own otherness. The feeling that *"Jesus understands me - maybe he was somehow like me"* can be healing. On the other hand, this projection also causes anxiety - for some believers, the questioning of a familiar (masculine-ascetic) image of Jesus is disturbing. This reveals a tension between the need for *identification* and the fear of *changing the image of God.*

## Thinking of Jesus as queer: theological and spiritual implications

So what does it mean *theologically, spiritually* and *in terms of church policy* to think of Jesus as *queer*? First of all, it does not mean defining Jesus in terms of a modern sexual identity, but rather taking him seriously *as a transgressor of boundaries.* Theologically, this is based on the conviction that Christ is the liberator *of all* people - and thus also transcends the norms of gender and sexuality that marginalize people.

When God becomes human in Jesus, it is in full solidarity with the diversity of humanity. The *incarnation* encompasses everything human, including physicality and eroticism. *"If Jesus was fully human, then he must have been fully erotic,"* concludes Shore-Goss - and in a good way. Because what God accepts in Christ is *redeemed.* Thus, a sexual dimension of Jesus would mean that *sexuality - regardless of orientation* and sensation - is something fundamentally good and blessed by God, part of the *imago Dei*, the image of God.

Spiritually, the idea of a queer Jesus opens up new approaches for many people: those who perceive themselves as *different* could more easily believe that God's love is also for them if even Jesus was *"different"* and *"diverse"*. Jesus becomes a *brother in otherness*, a divine companion through experiences of being an outsider. Shore-Goss believes that Jesus, as a queer individual, could empathize with the struggle of gay men, for example - feeling *"like outcasts"* and victims of violence because of their way of loving. Indeed, Jesus suffered marginalization and violence even though (or because) he challenged norms.

In terms of church politics, a queer Christology offers options for adaptation. If Jesus subverted heteronormative expectations, churches that refer to him would have to welcome all people regardless of their sexuality and gender relationships. *Inclusivity* becomes the imperative of discipleship. A church that continues to discriminate should ask itself whether it is *really* acting in the spirit of Jesus.

For example, the *#OutInChurch* initiative - an association of queer church workers in Germany - argues in its manifesto: *"A church that invokes Jesus and his message must take a firm stand against all exclusion"*. Queer theologians see Jesus as an *ally* of those who stand outside traditional norms. In terms of church policy, this means no longer using Christ as the guarantor of a rigid heavenly order (*"Jesus wanted marriage to be only between a man and a woman..."*), but rather as a *source of constant renewal* - which calls for a progressive, progressive community. After all, many common images of Jesus - the social reformer, the suffering servant, etc. - were also the result of certain historical contexts.

According to the proponents, a *queer perspective* on Jesus is therefore *no less legitimate* than other contextualizations, but can be theologically enriching. It sheds light on aspects of Jesus' message that have previously been underestimated: comprehensive inclusion, love relationships beyond convention, criticism of religious narrow-mindedness. Spiritually, this can lead to a deepened Christ-mysticism, in which Jesus truly *becomes "all things to all people"* (cf. 1 Cor 9:22) -

including queer people as their savior. It invites believers to question their own categories and to encounter God in new, surprising forms.

## Changing image of God: fluid, physical, non-binary

When we think of Jesus - the *image of the invisible God* (Col 1:15) - in a queer way, our image of God inevitably changes. God then appears less as a static, patriarchal ruler and more as a *fluid mystery* that reveals itself in many different ways. In fact, the Christian tradition has long emphasized that God *himself* is beyond gender. Church father *Gregory of Nyssa* (4th century) taught that the true image of God in man does not lie in sexual difference, but in the spiritual ability to have communion with God.

Nevertheless, the idea of God as a *man* (Old Father, male Jesus) has shaped our piety - often to the exclusion of female and queer dimensions. Queer theology builds on feminist images of God here, but goes even further. It invites us to think of God in images that embrace *physicality and diversity*. If Jesus as a human being perhaps desired and loved, then God is not without passion either. Althaus-Reid even speaks of the *holiness of the indecent*: The *sacred* and the physically sensual should no longer be separate. God is then no longer just the distant untouchable, but the *"God with us"* who dwells in our kisses and embraces - *"present in the love-lust of the marginalized"*.

Such an image of God *expands binary concepts*. It is *non-binary* in the sense that God is not defined as male *or* female, but reflects all genders. There are points of reference for this in the Bible itself: God as a mother (Is 66:13), as a midwife (Ps 22:10), as a wise woman (Prov 8) - and Jesus, who wants to protect Jerusalem in a motherly way like a hen (Mt 23:37). When God became man, God also blessed *human sexuality* in its entirety.

Queer Christology therefore emphasizes the *corporeality of God*: in Jesus, God took on a body that knew hunger, pain, joy and perhaps also erotic attraction. This contradicts a spiritualized image of God and places the dignity of the body at the center of theology. *Theology itself is a sexual act*, Althaus-Reid exaggeratedly formulated - namely to the extent that our physical and sensual existence is always involved in the theological quest.

A fluid, body-centered image of God can help believers to feel at home in God, even with their queer bodies. It broadens the view: God is bigger than our pigeonholes, *transcends gender boundaries as well as sexual orientations and identities* and at the same time encompasses all concrete forms of love in which people find each other.

## Opportunities for a queer Christology: identification, inclusion, liberation

A queer view of Jesus opens up *new opportunities for* the church and theology. On the one hand, it promotes *identification*: people who previously felt marginalized can recognize themselves in Jesus. A gay Christian can think: *Jesus understands my love*, a trans* person: *Christ knows what it is like to be misunderstood*. By seeing Jesus in solidarity as a *queer brother*, faith becomes more personal and existential.

Secondly, *inclusion* is growing. If all human diversity is already accepted in Jesus, there must be no exclusion in his church. The message *"do not be afraid"* then also applies to gender and sexuality. Parishes could be more open to LGBTQIA+ members and no longer deny sacraments and blessings to anyone on the basis of identity or orientation. Such a church would be truly *Catholic* in the literal sense - all-inclusive.

Thirdly, a queer Christology holds enormous *liberating potential*. It can liberate believers from false shame and self-destructive denial. Many LGBTQIA+ Christians have suffered from feeling or being told that their faith and identity are incompatible. However, if all sexualities are recognized as *"an inherited blessing"* - *"for we are made in God's image"*, as Shore-Goss points out - then the burden of sin and shame falls from the shoulders of those affected. Moreover, this also enables *heterosexual* believers to gain a more positive view of their own bodies and sexuality, free from the fear of doing something *"impure"*.

Theologically, the queer perspective leads back to the central message of *God's love*: unconditional acceptance of *all* people. The church would be true to its own teaching if - according to James Alison - it finally stopped cynically and inhumanely scapegoating certain groups and instead welcomed all people in their full identity.

*Figure2 : Jesus Christ queer.*

*A colorful painting of Jesus Christ in a modern, symbolic interpretation. Jesus raises his right hand in blessing, while his left hand rests on his heart, which is painted in rainbow colors and crowned by a cross. A large rainbow halo shines behind him. The vibrant rainbow colors emphasize themes of love, acceptance and inclusion, especially of course with regard to the LGBTQIA+ community. The artistic style is vibrant, expressive and symbolizes an inclusive, contemporary and open religious message.*

A *queer Christology* is in continuity with other liberation movements in theology: just as *black theology* emphasized Jesus' identification with the oppressed on the basis of skin color, *queer theology* emphasizes his identification with those marginalized on the basis of gender/orientation. In both cases, it is about the experience: *"God is on our side"*, which unleashes an immense power for liberation and reconciliation. Queer Christology can thus be understood in terms of *the history of salvation*: God is always revealing new facets of his love in order to call ever new groups into community. At the same time, it is not a special topic "only for queers". It generally teaches that *diversity enriches*.

By challenging rigid norms, the whole church can understand more deeply what it means to be one body in Christ (1 Cor 12) - with many different members. After all, Jesus himself encouraged diversity among his followers (from Zealots to tax collectors, from fishermen to scholars, from men to women). Why should his church in the 21st century be poorer than his circle of disciples 2000 years ago?

## Conservative objections in the modern age

Of course, there are also *conservative objections* to the idea of a queer Jesus. From a classical orthodox perspective, any claim that Jesus had homoerotic relationships *is speculative and unbiblical*. The Gospels are silent on Jesus' sexuality - and this silence is interpreted by traditional theologians as a sign that Jesus had *no sexual relationships whatsoever*, neither with men nor with women. In the early church, he was regarded as the *new Adam*, who was without sin; for many, this implicitly excludes sexual activity - at least outside of marriage. Accordingly, a "queer" interpretation is rejected as *an anachronistic projection* of modern categories into the Bible. A frequent accusation is that queer theology *bends* the scriptures in order to adapt them to today's knowledge and ways of being, and distorts the person of Jesus in the process. But perhaps homoerotic feelings 2000 years ago were no different to those of someone today who is about to come out.

Conservative critics fear that the uniqueness of Christ - such as his purity and self-giving - will be lost through such interpretations. They ask: should Jesus now be made the *object of identification for every minority*? Was he then also black, poor, disabled, queer, etc.? From their point of view, there is a danger of reducing Jesus to a human characteristic and obscuring his universal role as savior. Even if a universal role includes queers and others. It is also argued that Jesus' primary message was of a spiritual nature (repentance, kingdom of God), not the abolition of (then) social norms: That Jesus was not married was an expression of his special mission - not his "queerness".

From a Catholic perspective, much also hinges on Jesus' *male identity* - only because Jesus was male, so the argument goes, could ordination to the priesthood be restricted to men; a Jesus who *gender fluidity* would allow such doctrinal constructs to adapt to openness in interpretation.

These objections are a reminder that for many believers, the figure of Jesus is linked to personal piety when they first get to know him - changes here understandably trigger uncertainty. Every new interpretation must therefore be communicated sensitively in educational lessons by those who have already been socialized if we do not want to deepen the hardening of unlearned patterns of thought, action and understanding in the church.

## Talk about it openly and without fear - in educational work

In view of possible controversial positions and the need to broaden horizons through educational work, it is all the more important to discuss the question of whether Jesus can be thought of as queer *in an open, fearless and respectful* manner. Theological faculties and congregations are called upon to create a framework in which such topics are neither tabooed nor polemically distorted. *Encouraging open discussion* means first of all: recognizing these questions as *legitimate theological* questions, not dismissing them as provocation. No one should have to fear being suspected of heresy just because they think about Jesus' sexuality. Pastors or lecturers can make it clear: Talking about it is not sacrilege, but part of our effort to understand Jesus as a true human being.

*Educational work* is also important: many reservations are based on ignorance of the historical background or biblical texts. Theologians should proactively introduce the relevant biblical passages and research findings into seminars and sermons so that different interpretations become known. For example, the figures of the *"beloved disciple"* or the centurion-servant could be considered together in a congregational Bible study, without making an immediate value judgment, but asking: What could this mean? When believers learn that even the church fathers argued about Jesus' full humanity and mystics saw feminine traits in Jesus, they realize that our questions are not completely out of thin air.

A further step is the *decoupling of sexuality and guilt*. As long as sexuality remains something dirty in the church's subconscious, people will be reluctant to talk about Jesus' sexuality. That's why we need a theological foundation that understands sexuality as a good, God-given part of being human - in line with the motto of creation: *"And behold, it was very good"* (Genesis 1:31).

For example, a loving couple having an orgasm together: a number of modern theologians - such as *Eugene F. Rogers* in *Sexuality and the Christian Body* (1999) - emphasize that sexuality is an integral part of the image of God. When congregations internalize that sexuality *does not* automatically mean sin, the fear of talking about Jesus' sexuality disappears.

Finally, a *safe space* must be created: Pastors and teachers who facilitate such discussions (including online) deserve support.

A *church without fear* - the slogan of *#OutInChurch* - will only emerge if those responsible for leadership provide support instead of nipping reflective questions in the bud. When bishops and professors emphasize alongside pastors how important free questioning is for faith, a climate of trust is created.

The question *"Was Jesus queer?"* leads into an exciting subject area between biblical studies, theology and contemporary experience. It challenges us to rethink familiar images of Jesus and God - but this is precisely where we have the opportunity to delve deeper. A fluid, physical, non-binary image of God may be unsettling at first, but it can bring us closer to the *mystery of Christ*, who *"surpasses all knowledge"* (Ephesians 3:19).

If Jesus is truly human, we must not exclude anything human from him - not even the facets that seem unusual to us. And if God is truly love, then this love excludes no one.

A queer Christology invites us to rediscover the *vastness of God*. It can build bridges to those who have become alienated from the church and faith, and enrich the church with a more diverse, more colorful idea of the God who became man in Jesus. It is now up to all of us - laypeople and theologians alike, conservative and progressive - to enter into dialog without fear. In this dialog, we could ultimately learn more about Jesus - and about ourselves.

# Chapter 3:
# Eroticism and faith: Is celibacy an expression of freedom - or of fear of physicality?

*The chapter deals with celibacy, a central and controversial practice of the Catholic Church that obliges priests to remain celibate for life. Historically, celibacy was not an initial demand of the early church, but developed gradually out of spiritual, but also pragmatic and economic motives. Biblical texts do not offer clear support for compulsory abstinence, but emphasize the freedom to choose between marriage and celibacy. The current practice of compulsory celibacy has been shown to lead to serious psychological and social problems such as loneliness, emotional overload, double standards and an increased risk of psychosexual immaturity and abusive behavior among priests. Queer-feminist perspectives also criticize celibacy as an expression of a patriarchal, anti-body and anti-sexuality tradition that systematically marginalizes women and queer people. International Catholic practice already shows models of married priests today, which illustrates a fundamental flexibility and adaptability of the church. Many current theological voices, including Pope Francis, point to a possible reform of celibacy that focuses more on voluntariness and realism. The abolition of celibacy should and must also take place promptly in response to the numerous cases of child abuse by male priests.*

- ***Question:*** *How can the Catholic Church reform and abolish celibacy in such a way that it becomes an expression of genuine freedom instead of a psychological and social burden?*
- ***Question:*** *Isn't compulsory celibacy today an expression of a deep-seated fear of sexuality and physicality rather than a sign of true spiritual freedom?*
- ***Option for action:*** *The Catholic Church should abolish compulsory celibacy and instead - this is tantamount to*

abolishing choice - enable a voluntary way of life in which priests can freely decide whether they want to live celibately or enter into partnerships - this would significantly strengthen the credibility, authenticity and humanity of the Church.

- **Training option:** Clergy, believers and students in religious education should be comprehensively trained in their emotional intelligence and relational skills, for example through seminars on psychosexual development, communication, self-reflection and diversity-sensitive theology, in order to successfully implement the change towards an inclusive and credibly lived priestly identity.

Celibacy - the promise of celibacy: and thus a life of solitude without a relationship - has been considered a characteristic of the Catholic priesthood for centuries. Admirers see it as a voluntary renunciation out of deep freedom and devotion to God, while critics *see it as an expression of sexual hostility* and *fear of physicality*. They also see it as *an economic instrument of power*, so that priests' lavish salaries are not passed on to family members, but go back to the church in the event of death.

Current debates - such as the Synodal Path in Germany - have made the question of whether compulsory celibacy is still in keeping with the times highly topical. Even Pope Francis has expressed an open mind: The celibacy of priests *is "a temporary rule"* without an eternal character - in other words, not an indispensable dogma. At the same time, he warned that a mere renunciation of relationships could degenerate into *"comfortable loneliness"*.

This article sheds light on the topic of celibacy in a theologically sound and generally understandable way from various perspectives: from biblical origins and historical motives to psychological consequences and current reform ideas and proposals for change: the abolition of the abstinent solitude of the clergy. So is celibacy an act of free love for God - or does it stem from an internalized fear of the body and sexuality as well as economic constraints?

## Historical development of celibacy

*Origins in the early church:* In the first Christian centuries, there was *no general celibacy requirement* for priests. Many clergy - including high-ranking officials - were married; the New Testament even mentions that *apostles such as Peter had a mother-in-law.*

Tradition shows that married bishops, priests and deacons were a matter of course in early Christianity.

However, sexual abstinence soon began to be expected of clerics, at least some of the time, especially before celebrating religious services. This ideal was linked to ideas of *cultic purity* known from pre-Christian Jewish and pagan traditions - the idea that sexual activity made the priest "unclean" for the sacred already reflected a certain fear or at least skepticism towards physicality.

*Establishment in the Middle Ages*: Over the centuries, the recommendation changed into an obligation. Regional synods such as Elvira (around 306) demanded abstinence from married clerics, but celibacy only became binding for the entire Western Church in the *High Middle Ages*. At the Lateran Councils of 1123 and 1139, celibacy was declared a *prerequisite* for ordination to the priesthood. Married clergy were even required to *dissolve* their marriage - a drastic step that shows how absolute the ideal had become.

There were various motives behind this enforcement: on the one hand, spiritual reasons - Jesus' words about the *"eunuchs for the sake of the kingdom of heaven"* (Mt 19:12) and the conviction that a priest should devote himself undividedly to God and the Church were invoked. On the other hand, there were also very pragmatic considerations: *Questions of inheritance and power politics* played a part. As a priest died without legitimate descendants, his property fell to the church - not to a family. Celibacy therefore also secured ecclesiastical influence and financial interests. In the Reformation period at the latest, celibacy was also stylized as a distinguishing feature compared to Protestants, who allowed priests to marry. Despite occasional criticism (e.g. during the Enlightenment), the Catholic Church adhered to compulsory celibacy and reaffirmed it in the 20th century (Pope Pius XII and the Second Vatican Council confirmed the value of the celibate priesthood).

*No primordial Christian necessity:* Historically, it is therefore clear that compulsory celibacy was a *disciplinary development - not* a law ordered by Jesus. Accordingly, the Second Vatican Council made it clear that celibacy was *"not demanded by the nature of the priesthood itself"*. It is therefore *not dogmatically binding,* but is a church commandment that has arisen in the course of history. This fact is significant: what has become historical can, in principle, also be changed again historically. This is exactly what many are calling for today - a return to the fact that celibacy should be *a self-chosen option*, but not the only way of life for priests.

## Biblical foundations and early practice

The *Holy Scriptures* provide an ambivalent picture of the question of marriage versus celibacy. Jesus himself hardly says anything about it - he presumably lived a celibate *life, but never demanded this of all his disciples*. On the contrary: several apostles were married (Peter, presumably others too). The Pastoral Epistles even state that a bishop should be *"the husband of one wife"* (cf. 1 Tim 3:2) - which at least implies that married ministers were normal. The oft-quoted passage from Matthew 19:12 (of those *"who have made themselves unfit for marriage for the sake of the kingdom of heaven")* and *Paul's advice in 1 Corinthians 7* have been used in the tradition as the biblical basis for singleness. Paul does indeed recommend singleness out of his personal calling (*"I wish all men were like me"*), but at the same time he emphasizes that this is *not a command from the Lord*, but advice that everyone should live according to their gift of grace (cf. 1 Cor 7:7 and 7:25). He recognizes the value of both vocations - marriage *and* singleness - as different gifts from God. The Bible *does not* literally *state an inferior value of marriage, nor a general superiority of virginity*. Rather, the New Testament shows that love and devotion to Christ can be lived in different ways.

Early Christian church orders then also show a *coexistence:* married priests lived with their families and served the church, while at the same time the emerging *ascetic movement* (monasticism) praised voluntary virginity out of respect for the coming kingdom of God. This tension is still reflected today: official church documents praise celibacy as *"appropriate in many respects"* to the priesthood and as a *sign of the coming, heavenly world*. At the same time, however, they emphasize that marriage and celibacy complement each other. *From a theological point of view, both states of life are valid ways of serving God.* Genesis already points out that man and woman should be fruitful in marriage (Gen 1:28), and the letter to the Hebrews calls marriage *"honorable"* (Heb 13:4). The Bible knows many holy spouses. According to biblical understanding, it is *not sexual abstinence per se* that is decisive for a life pleasing to God, *but love, justice and mercy*. In other words: Anyone who is married and acts in love is not inferior to an abstainer in the kingdom of heaven - and a celibate person without love misses the mark just the same. This balance was sometimes lost sight of in later centuries when the virginal way of life was idealized as a *"higher state"*. However, such hierarchical thinking is hardly based on the Bible.

## Psychological and social effects on priests today

How does compulsory celibacy affect the reality of life for today's priests? Many studies and field reports paint a mixed picture. There are priests who see their celibacy as a liberation - they feel *undividedly there for God and people*, have deep friendships and a fulfilled spiritual life. However, there are also numerous voices that point out the *downsides*: Loneliness, inner conflicts and sometimes double lives.

*Loneliness and isolation:* Priests often complain of loneliness and a feeling of being alone, especially in old age.

Wunibald Müller, theologian and psychotherapist, reports from his many years of supporting priests that celibacy leaves many with a strong feeling of *not being loved*. This often intensifies in retirement when active parish work ceases. In 2017, a group of older priests from Cologne wrote an open letter in which they named *loneliness as a pressing problem* and called for an open debate about celibacy. Müller explains that the *"often unchosen loneliness"* leads to isolation and the natural *need for togetherness* remains unfulfilled. Some seek substitute satisfactions - e.g. excessive eating, drinking or escaping into virtual sexuality - to compensate for their inner emptiness. Sexual abuse of children and young people in the church by male priests should also be discussed in this context. Such observations show what a psychological burden the claim to live alone represents for many a pastor.

*Double lives and "secret" relationships:* Another phenomenon is the widespread *double standard* that compulsory celibacy can lead to. Quite a few priests enter into intimate relationships - only in secret, for fear of consequences. *Secret partnerships* are not uncommon; some priests have children who are not officially allowed to exist. A drastic example: In France, the illegitimate son of a priest was disowned by his own father instead of standing by him. Such cases - documented in the ARTE film *"Celibacy - The Catholic ordeal"* - show how agonizing the situation can be for everyone involved. Clergymen who fall in love are faced with the decision of either keeping the relationship secret (with a guilty conscience) or giving up their vocation. Many initially opt for the former - a life of conflict. *"Secret relationships, troubles of conscience and disowned children are among the side effects of compulsory celibacy,"* one report aptly states.

Over time, however, many leave this double life and resign from the ministry because they can no longer stand the games of hide-and-seek. As a result, the church loses committed pastoral workers - while those who stay may be caught up in internal conflicts or hypocrisy. According to Pope Francis, an internal Vatican study found that it *is better to end a double life than to continue it*, especially with regard to homosexual priests. This drastic advice underlines how real the problem of double lives and homophobia still is. Homosexual clerics would rather be thrown out of the nest than be allowed to suffer psychological distress induced by the church itself.

A very perfidious, discriminatory and toxic, even pathological and inhuman system that prefers the (professional and thus also identity-related) erasure of existence through removal from the system to tolerated hypocrisy - a study consultant:Inside team with separating recommendation, if one understands identity erasure in the social and removal from the profession as a recommendation: the "do-it-yourself-away" as induced "go- prefer-it-yourself" recommendation is simply a degressive personnel policy: a paradigm of a subtle ejection mentality.

Does such a general recommendation and way of thinking possibly show and convey an attitude of the team of consultants of said internal study that could be metaphorically and cinematically pointed out as a 'Kill Bill' recommendation? (In Quentin Tarantino's film of the same name, the protagonist, who wanted to start a new life together and get married, was brutally attacked by the boss "Kill Bill" on the day of the wedding preparations - and all her friends and guests were murdered).

David Berger's homosexuality as a Vatican advisor and later book author is a prime example of the removal of a person from the community who may have implemented such recommendations in personal and work processes and personnel policy - even if or precisely because many ultimately (have to) resign from their job and vocation. And that is simply not possible: even a heterosexual priest has the right to remain in office, or to opt for the desired secrecy, if he was allowed to experience the joy of true and lasting love for a neighbor.

Does the head of the church have the right advisors and directors of studies? The recommendation to 'seek your own salvation and then please work as a cashier in the supermarket (instead of pretending to be in church)' could perhaps be seen as well-intentioned advice. In reality, however, this attitude should be seen as systematic bullying in the workplace, aimed at persuading affected employees to voluntarily give up their job.

So what does it mean to *"end a double life rather than continue it in church work*, especially with regard to homosexual priests" or priests who are about to become fathers and have broken celibacy? - Is it a recommendation to leave the church or even a recommendation to end one's (professional and therefore also social) life? - It is alarming that such recommendations from study advisors are still circulating today or could even be supported by the pope: "Find your happiness somewhere outside the church system, but don't pretend to be celibate with us - even if it means ostracizing yourself professionally". This persistent discrimination against homosexual clergy or clergy in relationships (including heterosexual ones), supported by the rigid adherence to celibacy, is in fact an attack on their professional identity and personal integrity. Rather, it would be necessary to address the root causes that cause such discriminatory structures and a life of induced hypocrisy to the point of self-abandonment - resulting in a recommendation to abolish celibacy.

A personnel policy stance that recommends a mentality of exclusion is not justifiable even in regular work organizations. The exclusion of employees from work processes can only ever be an individual last *resort for* an organization. Under no circumstances should it become a general recommendation or even a paradigm of a leader in order to establish an organizational culture of rejection or even a culture of disgust through induced remorse in order to remove oneself through deliberately created feelings of guilt or shame. This non-compliance on the part of leading teachers and practitioners would be undignified and contemptuous of life and humanity. In a church context, who would confide in such a leader about wanting to marry their boyfriend or care for their soon-to-be-born child?

*Emotional overload and risk of abuse:* the psychosexual immaturity of some priests can have a particularly serious impact. Experts emphasize that a healthy integration of one's own sexuality is part of human maturity - if this is made more difficult by a taboo, personality disorders can be encouraged Stephan Buttgereit, Co-Chairman of the Synodal Forum *"Priestly Existence Today"*, for example, warns: *"Wherever people are not aware of their sexual identity, dangers lie dormant".* In particular, *"regressively immature"* personalities among clergy can arise due to the tabooing of sexuality - and this immaturity *encourages abuse*, according to perpetrator profiles from a church study. The MHG study published by the German Bishops' Conference in 2018 found evidence that strict church sexual morals and the celibate lifestyle contribute in some cases to repressed sexuality, which can then be unleashed in unhealthy ways. Although celibacy is not the cause of the abuse problem, the researchers noted that an immature approach to one's own body and desire is a risk factor. Excessive ascetic ideals can therefore turn into the opposite in the worst case. The *appearance of holiness* is of little help if human needs are fermenting behind it that cannot find constructive expression. In fact, in church history, an *exaggerated idealization of celibacy* has *often led to hypocrisy, double lives or even abuse.* This scientific observation warns us that outward abstinence is no guarantee of inner freedom - on the contrary, forced renunciation without a genuine vocation can have a destructive effect.

Compulsory celibacy can therefore become a heavy burden if it is not truly borne out of inner freedom. Many priests master it - but many also suffer noticeably as a result. The psychological and social consequences range from *loneliness* and *double standards* to *psychological crises*. This reality challenges the church to take an honest look: Does the law of celibacy really always serve the salvation of pastors and the faithful? Or does it produce avoidable suffering and contradictions?

# Queer-feminist perspectives

From a queer-feminist perspective, compulsory celibacy is once again examined in a different way. The focus here is on questions of *gender justice, sexual morality* and power structures. Feminist theologians and queer theologians emphasize that the ideal of the celibate male priest is deeply rooted in a *patriarchal culture* that has long held physicality and female sexuality in particular in low esteem.

*So far, no participation of women:* For Catholic women, the fact that the priesthood and celibacy have historically been linked presents a double barrier. They cannot become priests - and therefore the question of celibacy does not arise for them in this form, unless they choose the path of religious life. Some church historians continue to point out that one of the purposes of celibacy was to maintain a *closed society of men*. By not allowing priests to have wives and families, women were effectively kept out of the immediate environment of the clergy. This promoted a male-dominated church hierarchy in which women had little place. The pejorative ideas of medieval theologians - such as women as "seductresses" and marriage as a venial concession to weakness - resonate in the idea of celibacy.

Queer-feminist criticism sees this as a *fear of female corporeality* that has been spiritually exaggerated. The compulsory celibacy of all priests could be seen as an institutionalized expression of this fear. As Hubert Wolf explains, priestly celibacy was often *spiritually glorified* and ultimately justified with an ideology of cultic purity. However, there was no word of Christ behind this, but rather ancient ascetic ideals and misogyny: women were seen as a threat to purity, sexuality as a driving force to be curbed. Feminist theologians, on the other hand, call for a *theology of body-friendliness* that values sexuality as an integral part of being human and of creation - for both men and women. From such a perspective, a celibacy requirement seems like an anachronism from a time that was hostile to the body.

*From a queer theological perspective*, celibacy is also closely linked to traditional Catholic sexual morality, which recognizes *heterosexual marriage as the only legitimate place for sexuality*. For non-heterosexual people (whether priests or laypeople), this effectively meant a lifelong ban on chastity, as they were previously not allowed to marry or live a partnership and togetherness. Many LGBTQIA+ people experienced and still experience the church's demand for abstinence as deeply unjust - as if their ability to love was being *negated*. Queer theologians ask: Is it really God's will for a person to suppress their love and sexuality just because it doesn't fit the heteronormative mold? That would be like Tim Thaler selling his laughter to the devil in the children's series of the same name. There are numerous *homosexual priests* in the church ministry, many of whom hide their orientation for fear of sanctions. This in turn leads to the double standards already mentioned above , which Pope Francis addressed: *"It is better for them to resign the priesthood than to lead a double life,"* he said about secretly active homosexual clerics - certainly with the best moral intentions, even if abandonment (with the exclusion of one option (being able to marry as a priest)) is the then enforced solution of self-flagellation. So he did not - yet - say: it is better: if they marry and remain in the profession

Queer perspectives object: Wouldn't it be better to openly accept that there are also queer priests with partnerships instead of forcing them into a double life? If celibacy were voluntary, or if togetherness in partnership could also apply to priests, queer priests would no longer necessarily *have* to love in secret or renounce love.

The following also applies to heterosexual priests: *love is not a luxury, but a central part of being human.* Queer-feminist voices insist that the church must finally recognize that *eroticism and faith are not mutually exclusive*, but can enrich each other. Theologian *Doris Reisinger* (herself a former nun) writes that it is no coincidence that an institution with a male-dominated, celibate leadership structure has such major problems in dealing with sexuality and abuse - a *"theology of fear"* of sexuality has prevailed for centuries, but now it is time for a *theology of love*. Not everyone puts it so gracefully, but the tenor is clear: a system based on fear, control and exclusion must give way to an inclusive view. *"Questions that used to be answered at the stake are now asked freely in religious education"*, as the first volume of *"Deus ex Machina"* put it.

This ever-present freedom to ask questions - for example about the role of women, about the recognition of queer partnerships - requires answers from the church, and even critics of a questioning life cannot deny this. In fact, reform efforts are often met with *resistance for fear of losing power*. Some people in the hierarchy may unconsciously think: *"I had to struggle, so others shouldn't have it easier now"*. But such personal motives must not be allowed to determine the development of the church, advocates of reform demand.

From a queer-feminist perspective, the answer is therefore more likely to be: *celibacy (today) stems more from a fear of physicality than genuine freedom*. It is symbolic of an oppressive sexual morality that marginalizes women and LGBTQIA+ people. A truly humane and just church must overcome this fear and recognize loving relationships - whether hetero or queer - as intended by God. Accordingly, there is a call to break the strict link between ordination and abstinence in order to create space for *all* those who want to serve the church without denying their God-given capacity for love.

## Celibacy in the light of contemporary anthropology

Today's theology and anthropology emphasize *the human being as a unity of body and spirit*. The body is not merely an appendage of the soul, but an integral part of the person - created by God and *"very good"* (Genesis 1:31). In this light, the question arises: does a model of life that completely excludes the sexual dimension still fit in with our current understanding of what it means to be human? Is celibacy a sign of radical freedom, because someone can do without something good - or does it testify to an outdated view of humanity that separates body and soul?

*Body-friendliness instead of hostility towards the body:* modern Christian anthropology is *body-friendly*. In *Amoris Laetitia*, for example, Pope *Francis* emphasizes the positive significance of physical, erotic love within marriage: this is by no means a *"tolerated evil"*, but rather a gift from God that beautifies the encounter between the (married) partners.

Sexuality, properly understood, is an expression of love and *is itself* a gift from God. If the Church teaches this for married couples, how does it convey that the exact opposite should be the ideal for priests? There is an area of tension here. Theologically, it is argued that the priest is already *prophetically* living the coming reality in which people *"will no longer marry"* (cf. Mt 22:30). However, this eschatology must not obscure the *goodness of creation in the here and now* . More recent theological voices, including from the mouths of the magisterium, also relativize old exaggerations: We should *not diminish the value of marriage in order to increase celibacy*, Francis warns, citing John Paul II.

Both ways of life are different, but complement each other; in no way is one *per se* holier than the other. This brings a more balanced view into focus: celibacy can be a solitary and *charismatic way of life* that can arise from an authentic vocation - but it does not automatically make priests holier or better than married colleagues in twos. The decisive factor is the inner attitude.

*Relationship ethics and love as a vocation*: From an anthropological perspective, the urge for interpersonal love, partnership and family is part of human nature. The Catholic Church therefore regards marriage as a sacrament, as a path to holiness blessed by God. When a person receives the priesthood, why should they automatically be *excluded* from this form of vocation to love? Theologians argue that there can be two equivalent vocations: that of priestly ministry and that of marriage. They do not have to be mutually exclusive. An *ethic of relationship* would recognize that a priest in a mature relationship can live just as responsibly, lovingly and selflessly as a celibate priest does in this way of life. Love - be it *agape* for the next person or *eros* for the other person - is a vocation and a mission in both cases. Many saints of the past (e.g. St. Francis de Sales) emphasized that a good husband and father serves God just as much as a monk. Today we are reminded that *love is the greatest vocation*. It follows that priests who love (and marry) can also live their respective vocations - perhaps even in a more balanced way and closer to people.

*Freedom and motive test:* Celibacy only makes sense if it is *freely chosen* for the right motives. Anthropologically, a forced renunciation that goes against a person's inner nature would be problematic. A distinction can be made here between a genuine ascetic vocation and *"false asceticism"*. In the last volume *Deus Ex Machina*, it was already made clear that asceticism can become a facade if it is lived out of pressure, fear or a sense of duty. Signs *of misunderstood* abstinence are, for example, *contempt for the body* (seeing the body or sex as "unclean") or a tendency to judge others who do not follow this path.

Unfortunately, this is exactly what often happened: Some celibate clerics looked down on others *"living in sin"* with moral arrogance - a behavior that Jesus himself criticized in the Pharisees.

*Figure3 : A cheerful, not lonely priest with his family, wife and child .*

*A harmonious and warmly lit photograph depicting a family scene with a Catholic priest. The priest lovingly holds the hands of his smiling wife, while a happy young child stands between them, joyfully observing the interaction. The scene takes place outdoors in front of a church in the background, creating an atmosphere of security, closeness and familial connection. The picture subtly addresses aspects such as family, celibacy, human closeness and the discussion about reforms within the Catholic Church: it is about the abolition of celibacy, the loneliness of priests and thus the possibility and obligation of priests to be able to talk about the love of a relationship and lived togetherness, to have experienced it themselves.*

A modern, healthy anthropology of sexuality rejects such dualisms. It sees sexuality as integrative: those who accept themselves, also in their sexuality, can love and encounter others more authentically. This applies to priests and laypeople alike. This is why many theologians advocate *demystifying and abolishing* celibacy: It is *a possible* way of following Christ, but not a higher or necessary way. And a way of life does not have to be prescribed. The *holiness* of priests is not measured by their marital status, but by how someone leads their life with love, faith and dedication. As a Council text puts it, celibacy can be *"appropriate to the priesthood"*, *but it cannot be its essence*. In other words, priests can live celibate lives - but do not *have to* be or remain celibate to be good priests.

Overall, today's anthropology challenges the church to take a *reality check*: does the ideal of celibate priests still correspond to a positive image of humanity? Or does it reflect an outdated *fear of sexuality*? There is much to suggest that the latter is the case, at least as far as the obligatory aspect is concerned.

A life lived voluntarily in chastity for the sake of Christ can indeed be fulfilling and meaningful - but only if it is in harmony with the person. Where it is forced, it runs the risk *of hindering freedom instead of promoting it*. This is precisely why contemporary anthropologists and theologians are increasingly advocating *freedom of choice* in this area.

## International perspectives: married

A look at the universal church shows: Compulsory celibacy *is not a universal and irrevocable norm* in all Catholic rites. In the *Eastern churches* united with Rome (such as the Maronite, Melkite or Ukrainian Catholic churches), it has always been customary for people to marry before being ordained as priests - priests with wives and children are normal there. Pope Francis likes to refer to this tradition to show that married priests exist *"without problems"* in the church. The Orthodox churches also handle compulsory celibacy in this way. This means *that there are already Catholic priests with families today*, namely in the Eastern Churches and in some special cases in the Western Church.

*Converts:* Even in the Latin (Roman Catholic) Church itself, there have been and still are exceptions to the celibacy requirement. This is particularly noticeable in the case of former Anglican or Protestant pastors who convert to Catholicism: Some of them have been subsequently *ordained* as Catholic priests, *even though they are married.*

Since Benedict XVI, there have been personal ordinariates for former Anglicans in which a number of married priests work - in fact alongside celibate colleagues. These exceptions confirm the rule and at the same time show their relativity: apparently, a married priest is compatible with the Catholic understanding of ministry *after all*, even if so far only as a special case. It has long been known that Rome has ordained individual Lutherans or Anglicans after conversion. Married priests from the East were also occasionally appointed to pastoral care for Catholic parishes in Western Europe. The reality of the world church is therefore more diverse than the strict Roman Canon 277 suggests.

The Codex Iuris Canonici (CIC), i.e. the ecclesiastical code of the Roman Catholic Church, lays down the rules on celibacy for clergy in canon 277. Here is the translated wording of §1 in the current version (as of 2024) *The clergy are bound to perfect and perpetual continence for the sake of the kingdom of heaven and are therefore celibate.*

§ 2 states: *The clergy should not maintain too close a relationship with persons whose company may cause offense and should avoid staying in such places.*

*Canon 277* of the church's code of law therefore obliges Catholic clerics to complete and permanent abstinence, and therefore also social abstinence. Today, this regulation is being reflexively questioned in many contexts - both within the Church and from a social, psychological and human rights perspective.

In a modern, secular society, sexuality is seen as an integral part of human identity and relationship skills. Many see this as an *unnecessary restriction* of personal freedom and life choices.

From a psychological point of view, the demand for lifelong abstinence is also problematic. It can create inner tensions, identity conflicts or double standards if the commitment is involuntary. Studies suggest that celibacy obligations - especially when combined with a relationship of power and dependency - can harbor *structural risks* that lead to misconduct or covert lifestyles.

The obligation to celibacy is also assessed reflexively from a human rights perspective. The right to partnership, marriage and family is an internationally recognized human right.

In addition, Pope Francis has repeatedly indicated that celibacy is not a divine rule, but a disciplinary law of the Church - and can therefore be changed in principle.

*Amazon Synod and viri probati*: The *2019 Amazon Synod* was also an important highlight. In view of the dramatic shortage of priests in remote regions of Amazonia, the majority of synod fathers voted in favour of ordaining proven married men (*viri probati* in Latin) as priests. Over 80% of the bishops spoke out in favor of opening up to this.

Bishop Erwin Kräutler, who worked for decades on the Xingu in Brazil, emphasized: *"The indigenous peoples do not understand celibacy"* - in their communities it is unimaginable that spiritual leaders remain single, so they would not find access to such a priestly image. The synod's proposal aimed to bridge this cultural gap and ensure the provision of the Eucharist. In countries such as *Papua New Guinea* and *South Africa*, bishops have raised similar questions as to whether married people can be ordained as priests in pastoral emergencies. It is clear that the strict obligation of celibacy is faltering under the pressure of real needs.

*Resistance and developments:* Of course, there are also reservations worldwide. Parts of the Curia and conservative believers in particular see any relaxation as a breach of the dam. When the German synod members officially asked the Pope to review compulsory celibacy in 2023, the Vatican initially reacted cautiously or even skeptically. A warning letter stated that reforms on this issue could be viewed hesitantly for fear of division.

Nevertheless, there is international movement on the issue. In many Protestant countries (e.g. Germany, Switzerland), Catholics are asking why there are no married priests *here*, when their Orthodox neighbors know them. In regions with many conversions (e.g. England, where many Anglican priests have become Catholic), married and celibate priests already live *side by side*. And the Eastern Churches remind us that our own Catholic Church can be plural. This global context urges us to recognize that voluntary celibacy would *not be a revolution*, but rather an adjustment to a plural reality that has long been practiced. This *inconsistency* is becoming increasingly difficult to communicate.

# Current voices from the church and theology

In recent years, prominent church representatives have been increasingly calling for a *change to celibacy* or at least signaling openness to a reassessment. Although Pope Francis himself emphasizes the value of the previous teaching on the celibate lifestyle, he has repeatedly made it clear that it is an *ecclesiastical discipline*, not a dogma of faith carved in stone. In an interview in 2023, when asked about the possible abolition of compulsory celibacy, he replied: *"Yes, yes."* He recalled the practice of the Eastern churches and called the Latin law of celibacy a temporary rule *"that has no eternal character"*.

The phrase "Yes, yes." sounds harmless at first glance, but depending on the tone of voice and situation, it can mean a lot. In German, it is highly context-dependent and is often used with an undertone that expresses far more than mere agreement.

- *Agreeing, but impatient / annoyed - Meaning:* "I've already understood", "You don't need to say it again"
  Example:
  A: "Don't forget to take out the trash."
  B: "Yes, yes..."
- *Ironic or doubtful - meaning:* "I don't believe you", "Of course... (certainly not)"
  Example:
  A: "I wrote the math test without studying."
  B: "Yes, yes... of course."
- *Neutral-confirming (rarer) - Meaning:* genuine but somewhat distanced agreement
  Example: "Yes, yes, that's true, you're right."

In many cases, "Yes, yes" *doesn't* just mean "Yes", but rather: *"Leave me alone", "I'm not in the mood for a discussion" or even: "Kiss my ass."*

This meaning comes through especially when the sentence is said with an annoyed, condescending or ironic tone of voice. In such a case, "Yes, yes" is actually a politely packaged rejection or a defensive reaction - a kind of verbal eye roll. It means: "It's okay, just stop talking", or more directly: "Save the comment, I'm not listening anyway."

This phrase often crops up in conversations when someone feels patronized or has no more nerve for further discussion. For example: If someone says *"You should really think about your behavior"* and the response is a snippy "Yes, yes...", then there is less insight behind it than rejection - in the sense of *"Fuck you"*, but with a certain social filter.

Depending on the tone of voice, "Yes, yes" can also mean: "I don't believe a word you say", "I don't care" or simply "Stop talking". It's one of those typical phrases where *the tone conveys the real message,* not the words themselves. And that's what makes them so ambiguous in everyday life - or so effective.

These words from the Pope's mouth were sensational for many observers and offered plenty of room for interpretation - even if Francis also doubted that an exemption from celibacy would automatically trigger a rush of vocations to the priesthood.

What is important is that the Pope *does not rule out a change*. This means that the door is open - albeit in wise consideration and in unity with the universal Church

And the questions and dialog continue: the topic was also discussed intensively at the German *Synodal Path*. The 2023 Synodal Assembly voted overwhelmingly in favor of asking the Pope *to review compulsory celibacy*. The text adopted states that "the link between the granting of ordinations and the obligation to remain celibate should be *re-examined"*.

An even more far-reaching demand - to ask the Pope directly to abolish celibacy - did not (yet) receive the necessary two-thirds majority, but the basic tenor was clear: the vast majority of German bishops and lay delegates definitely want a change. Interestingly, the synodal resolution also contains a request to examine whether *priests who have already been ordained* can be released from the promise of celibacy without giving up their ministry.

This is aimed at those priests who wish to enter into a relationship after years of service - a path back into active ministry should be open to them instead of them having to be laicized. The text of the resolution "The celibacy of priests - strengthening and opening up" received almost 95% approval. This almost unanimous vote from a section of the universal church is a strong signal.

Other bishops have also spoken out: in Switzerland, Bishop Jean-Marie Lovey suggested that the ordination *of married men* should be considered. In Amazonia, it is above all emeritus bishops such as Erwin Kräutler who have long advocated this. But there are also advocates in Europe.

In the meantime, the statements and demands have become more strident, fueled not least by the unspeakable and extensive *abuse crisis*. Cardinal Reinhard Marx, for example, said that there is *"no theological reason why celibacy and ordination must be inextricably linked"* - it is more important that priests are credible in their lives.

This creates a chorus of voices from different directions, along with many others: Pope Francis opens the door a crack, bishops and synod members push from within, theologians provide the justifications. Of course, there are still some defenders of the status quo who point to the beauty and spiritual value of celibacy. But overall, there are increasing signs that a change is possible.

# Opportunities of abolishing celibacy for a more humane church

What would change if celibacy were *abolished*? Numerous experts and those affected are hoping for positive effects for the church on various levels. Here are some possible opportunities of an *exemption* from celibacy - which, by the way, is equivalent to the abolition of celibacy - to decide freely for a partnership is also freedom:

- **More authenticity and fewer double standards:** If priests no longer had to live celibately against their will, the climate of honesty would grow. Secrets and double lives could be reduced, as no one would be forced to live their love in secret. Priests could be open about their relationships - as some clergy are already doing in exemplary fashion - without fear of sanctions. The church would gain *credibility* because it would not demand a way of life from its ministers that many cannot actually achieve without lying. The ideal would be for priests to *be fully human,* with all their emotions, and not have to suppress or hide anything. This also prevents dangerous inner conflicts that can lead to abuse or other aberrations. Overall, this would create a climate of greater *truthfulness.*

- **Pastors closer to people's lives:** Married or partnered priests share a lot with the faithful in terms of their lives: they know from their own experience about everyday marriage and family life, relationship work, perhaps also caring for children. This could make them *more competent and empathetic* in pastoral matters - e.g. in marriage and relationship counseling or youth pastoral care. Many Catholics would experience priests who have families themselves as more approachable. The *"image of priests"* would change: away from the solitary "spiritual master" towards compassionate fellow human beings who share the same joys and concerns. A more human church is characterized by clergy not standing on a pedestal of unattainable asceticism, but in the midst of people's lives. The renunciation of celibacy makes precisely this possible - because those who have the gift can remain celibate (and thus continue to give the sign of eschatology), but those who prefer to be celibate are particularly recognized in ministry.

- **Broader spectrum of vocations:** Without compulsory celibacy, significantly more people could consider a call to the priesthood. *Married* middle-aged people (e.g. permanent deacons or other committed people) could be considered for the priesthood, which would be particularly helpful in times of a shortage of priests.

In many congregations, there are proven family fathers with theological training who would perhaps take this step if permitted. *Young people* who have a profession of faith in their hearts but do not want to forgo a partnership and children of their own would also have an option. In addition, the ministry would be open to *queer people* who are currently effectively excluded if they do not want to deny their sexual orientation. An open-minded church that accepts priests with diverse lifestyles could (re)gain many committed believers who currently find themselves in stricter free churches or at a distance. The important thing is to do all this *without* losing the spirituality of the priests' ministry - after all, the Eastern churches and many Anglican communities practice exactly that and have by no means lost their spirituality.

It can even be an advantage: priests who are involved in family life may bring new spiritual accents to the church (keyword: house church, family services, etc.).

- **Improved mental health of clergy:** Many of the problems mentioned under "Psychological effects" above could be alleviated. The risk of loneliness in old age would decrease, as more priests with life partners would be less lonely. The burden of loneliness described by Wunibald Müller would be less pronounced.

It would also make the priesthood more attractive as a way of life for people with *normal emotional needs* - you would no longer have to appear "superhuman". The church would *step off the pedestal* and *into life*, so to speak, and admit it: Our priests:inside are people with heart and body, and that's a good thing. This can also counteract the inflated expectations of the faithful, who sometimes see priests as "different" beings. Overall, a culture could develop in which priests talk *more openly about personal issues* and seek advice when they struggle with abstinence, without having to fear breaking taboos.

- **Option for action: Focus on abolition**

In view of all these findings, many people have a vision for the future of the Catholic Church: make the voluntary nature of celibacy the focus of vocation ministry and thus abolish celibacy! In concrete terms, this means that young women and men - it can be assumed that the ordained ministry is open at the same time - should be encouraged to follow their spiritual vocation as priests - regardless of their relationship status.

- **Open up the priesthood to married and queer people:** Subsequently - and this is the vision of many queer-feminist theologians - one could also consider whether *all* people with a genuine vocation should be given access to the ministry, including those who are currently excluded: e.g. gay men in a partnership, or transgender people. Opening up the priesthood to **queer people** would mean that sexual orientation would no longer be a criterion for exclusion. Only the *integrity and suitability* of the person would be decisive, not their marital status or identity. This would be a big step towards an *inclusive church* in which diversity is seen as an enrichment.

The synodal process of the universal church (Synod 2021-2024) is already signaling in working documents that there is a desire to examine the issue of celibacy. The ball has been set in motion; now it is up to Rome and the bishops' conferences to take up the issue: a council could change the norm. Legally, it would be simple: Canon 277 CIC, which requires celibacy, would have to be deleted or reformulated. For example, a draft was formulated in the first volume of *Deus Ex Machina*: *"Clergy are free to choose whether they live alone, in partnership or in marriage, as long as their service to the Gospel is guaranteed."*

Instead of a church of fear, we want a church of *encounter and love*. In essence, it is about whether we trust God to work in a variety of ways. Can the Holy Spirit also call a father of a family to be a priest? Many believers say: Yes, he can - why should we slow him down? Can a priest credibly proclaim Jesus, even if he or she is in a same-sex partnership? If the relationship is lived in faithfulness and love, why not?

The end result is the realization that *the outward form - whether celibacy or marriage - does not determine holiness. The decisive factor is love.*

# Chapter 4:
# This is how the church marries same-sex love - and reinforces its own identity!

*The chapter deals with the question of whether and how the Catholic Church can marry then bless same-sex partnerships with the sacrament of marriage. For a long time, the Church categorically ruled out such weddings with the sacrament and blessing, but changed its position in part at the end of 2023 with the Vatican document "Fiducia supplicans". It now allows blessings for same-sex couples as long as it remains clear that these must not be confused with a sacramental marriage. For many believers, this decision means hope for more acceptance and inclusion, but at the same time raises questions as to why distinctions still need to be made between heterosexual and homosexual couples at all. Theologically, ethically and spiritually, many voices within the Church argue that same-sex partnerships live the same fundamental values of love, fidelity and responsibility as heterosexual relationships and therefore deserve the same liturgical forms of blessing. Internationally and pastorally, some local churches have already taken independent steps towards equal marriage with sacrament and blessing, which illustrates the growing approval and desire for liturgical equality.*

- *Question: How can the Catholic Church develop its theological foundations and pastoral practices to fully and completely include same-sex couples in its liturgical life?*
- *Question: Is a church that continues to make distinctions between the love of homosexual and heterosexual couples not in danger of denying Jesus' core message of unconditional love and acceptance?*
- *Option for action: The Catholic Church should completely abolish the distinction between heterosexual and homosexual couples in liturgical blessings and officially implement the same*

*liturgical rituals for the blessing and marriage of same-sex couples in order to credibly live out its pastoral credibility and inclusive claim.*

- **Training option:** *Clergy, believers and students in religious education should acquire skills in queer theology, intercultural sensitivity and ethical reflection, for example through workshops on inclusive or equalizing liturgy design and diversity-conscious interaction, in order to be able to authentically understand and credibly implement this theological change.*

*Figure4 : A rainbow over St. Peter's Basilica - a symbol of diversity and hope in the Catholic Church.*

*An impressive, atmospheric photo of St. Peter's Basilica in the Vatican under dramatic lighting. An intense, radiant rainbow stretches across the sky above the majestic architecture with its characteristic dome, symbolizing hope, diversity and change within the church. The scene is both imposing and symbolic, ideal for discussing inclusive theology with content on church reform, inclusion, diversity, peace and hope in religious and social contexts.*

Just a few years ago, the Vatican categorically ruled out blessings for homosexual couples. In February 2021, the Congregation for the Doctrine of the Faith declared that the Church had *"no authority to bless same-sex relationships"*, as such unions did not correspond to the Church's doctrinal plan. This prohibition, combined with the statement that sin could not be blessed, deeply offended many believers. They saw it as an affront.

## Current doctrinal developments: From prohibition to openness

However, a surprising turnaround followed in December 2023: In the Vatican declaration *Fiducia supplicans* ("The imploring trust"), a *first opening* was made. In it, Cardinal Victor Fernández, the new prefect of the authority for the faith, emphasized that the Church had *"expanded and enriched"* its understanding of blessing in light of Pope Francis' pastoral concerns.

Accordingly, *"the possibility now appears of being able to bless couples in irregular situations and same-sex couples without officially legitimizing their status or changing the Church's consistent teaching on marriage"*. It is also important to Rome to draw a distinction from marriage: confusion with a wedding ceremony must be ruled out. A blessing must not look like a wedding ceremony, must not take place at the same time as a civil marriage and must be explicitly different from the sacrament of marriage. Therefore, no fixed liturgical rituals should be introduced for such blessings in order to avoid equating them with marriage. Instead, the document speaks of *"spontaneous, non-ritualized"* blessings on a small scale - for example during a pilgrimage, a prayer meeting or in pastoral conversations.

Why heterosexual marriages should differ from homosexual marriages at the altar was not explained. The church is still stuck in the doctrine that same-sex couples are only couples, but not marriages. This is by no means the case, even if they can now legally enter into a marriage. Because: the love of two people is completely independent of their gender and/or sexual orientation.

The prayer of blessing is understood as a prayer for God's help, so that all that is good and true in the couple's life is placed under the assistance of the Holy Spirit. At the same time, the Vatican affirms that the traditional concept of marriage - the indissoluble union of man and woman, open to children - remains untouched, i.. continues to exist.

This opening nevertheless represented a balancing act: Without changing doctrine, the aim is to find pastoral ways of no longer rejecting loving couples outright. Georg Bätzing, Chairman of the German Bishops' Conference, expressly welcomed the Vatican's decision. He expressed *his gratitude for the pastoral perspective* of the document, as *same-sex couples and remarried divorcees* could now *be given a blessing*. In this way, the *"treasure" of the Church's diverse forms of blessing for the diversity of life models is "lifted up"* without calling sacramental marriage into question. These words show: From the perspective of reform-minded church representatives, opening up does not mean giving up Catholic identity, but rather a *further development of sacramental practice* in the service of people.

# Why rituals and sacraments do not have to be different

A liturgical ritual for the blessing and marriage of homosexual couples cannot and should not differ in essence from those for heterosexual couples. Both forms of partnership are based on the same theological, spiritual and human foundations: love, faithfulness, mutual support, public confession and trust in God's blessing. The differentiation of couples according to gender contradicts the biblical principle that before God, *people* are *not* judged *according to their outward appearance*, but according to their heart (cf. 1 Samuel 16:7; Galatians 3:28).

## Why the rituals do not have to be different:

1. **Theological reason:** The covenant that two people enter into in the presence of God is based on love, commitment and responsibility - regardless of gender.

2. **Ethical reason:** The equal value of all people requires equal liturgical forms of expression for equal relationships.

3. **Spiritual reason:** God's blessing is directed at people, not at gender roles. When two people unite in love, God's Spirit is in their midst (cf. Matthew 18:20).

4. **The common core of marriage:** love, mutual commitment, reliability, public witness, living faith in everyday life, a shared journey through life under God's guidance.

## Liturgical rituals for the blessing of a marriage (heterosexual and homosexual):

The classic liturgical elements of a church wedding ceremony, as they are customary in Protestant and Catholic contexts, are presented below - with information on how they can also apply to homosexual couples without modification.

### *Service to celebrate the love and blessing of the marriage of*

### *[name] & [name]*

## 1. opening and welcome: music and entry

**Content:** Entrance of the couple, greeting by the minister(s), introduction to the service.

**For same-sex couples:** Identical. They are greeted as *"bride and bridegroom"*, *"groom and groom"* or with neutral terms such as *"married couple in spe"*.

**Implementation:** Instrumental or vocal (e.. organ piece, favorite song of the couple, classical hymn such as "Praise the Lord" or modern song such as "A stone falls into the water"). The couple enters together or individually.

## 2. prayer and reading

**Content:** Prayer for God's presence; reading of a biblical text (e.g. 1 Corinthians 13, Song of Songs 8, Genesis 2).

**For same-sex couples:** Identical. Selection of texts according to life situation and theological orientation. The interpretation emphasizes universal statements of love and covenant.

### Implementation by liturgist:

*"In the name of God, the source of all life,*
*in the name of Jesus Christ, our brother and friend,*
*and in the name of the Holy Spirit, who unites us in love -*
*Welcome to this special service.*

*[Name] and [Name] are here today to celebrate their love for each other.*
*They want to place their life together under the blessing of God.*
*We celebrate with them, grateful and full of hope."*

### Realization in prayer:

*"Good God,*
*you give us fellowship, love and trust.*
*Be in our midst today,*
*bless [name] and [name] in their decision,*
*to walk their lives together.*
*Fill this room with your peace. Amen."*

## 3. scripture reading & sermon

**Content:** Interpretation of biblical texts in relation to love, faithfulness, responsibility, God's blessing.

**For same-sex couples:** Identical. Reference to the couple's love story, understanding of partnership and lived faith.

### Implementation in the scripture reading

**Possible texts:**

- *First Corinthians 13 ("Love is longsuffering...")*
- *Song of Songs 8:6-7 ("Place me as a seal on your heart...")*

- *Ruth 1:16 ("Where you go, there I will go also...")*
- *John 15:9-12 ("Love one another as I have loved you")*

*After the reading:*
*"Blessed are those who hear and keep God's word. Hallelujah."*

## Implementation with the sermon

## Key messages of a possible sermon:

- The love of two people is a gift from God.

- Loyalty, trust and commitment are signs of living discipleship.

- Same-sex love is just as much an expression of divine creation as any other form of partnership.

- Marriage is not a privilege of certain constellations, but a vocation to love - and therefore a sacred place.

### Example:
*"Dear congregation,*
*Two people stand before us today,*
*who want to make a promise to each other.*
*They are not doing this in secret, but visibly and with you as witnesses.*
*They trust that God will accompany their lives - in joy*
*in joy, in conflict, in everyday life, in hope.*

*The form of their love is no different from that of many others:*
*It is characterized by devotion, respect, tenderness and responsibility.*
*God has brought them together.*

*And we ask him: may he bless them."*

## 4. marriage question / wedding

**Content:** Public promise to love, respect and stand by each other - "until death do you part"

**For same-sex couples:** Identical. The wording is adapted: "Will you love and respect N., N..."

**Implementation by liturgist (to everyone):**

*"[Name], will you take [name] in marriage with a free heart,*
*love and respect him/her,*
*share life with him/her in good times and in hard times,*
*and remain faithful - as long as you live?"*

***Answer:** "Yes, with God's help."*

**Realization through wedding vows (free or traditional):**

*"I promise you,*
*to love, honor and respect you.*
*I want to accompany you and grow with you -*
*on good days and on difficult ones.*
*I want to be your home - for as long as we live."*

## 5. Ring exchange

**Content:** Ring exchange as a symbol of solidarity and loyalty.

**For same-sex couples:** Identical.

**Implementation by liturgist:**

*"The rings are signs of your love - round like the fidelity*
*that you promise each other. May they remind you of this every day."*

***On putting it on:***
*"[Name], I give you this ring -*
*as a sign of my love and loyalty."*

## 6. sacrament of marriage and blessing

**Content:** Laying on of hands, prayer for God's blessing for the couple and their future.

**For same-sex couples:** Identical. Here too, the act of blessing is an expression of divine accompaniment - not an evaluation of the genders.

**Implementation by priests:in:**

**Both kneel or stand next to each other. Laying on of hands.**

## Sacrament & blessing prayer:

*"Good God,
you have brought [name] and [name] together.
Bless them with your love.
Strengthen them in their patience and kindness.
Keep their love in times of darkness.
Fill them with joy and your spirit.
Let their love bear fruit -
for themselves and for all who meet them.
Amen."*

## 7. intercessions

**Content:** Prayers for the couple, the families, society, the church.

**For same-sex couples:** Identical. Possibly with an emphasis on the hope for comprehensive acceptance and integration.

**Implementation through exemplary intercessions (read by relatives or liturgist):**

*● We pray for [name] and [name],
that their love may grow and blossom,
that they may forgive each other,
that they remain a home for each other.*

*● We pray for the people
who long for love and are afraid to show it.
Let them also experience acceptance and blessing.*

*● We pray to you for our society and church:
For open hearts, just structures and courageous steps into the future.*

*All: "God, hear our prayer."*

## 8. the Lord's Prayer and final blessing

**Content:** Common prayer and mission under the blessing of God.

**For same-sex couples:** Identical.

## Implementation

> *"May the God of love bless you.*
> *May he keep you in fellowship with each other and with him.*
> *May he accompany you on your way - with joy, strength and comfort.*
> *May God bless you:*
> *The Father, the Son and the Holy Spirit.*
> *Amen."*

### 9. excerpt / music / celebration

**Content:** Conclusion of the service and beginning of the feast.

**For same-sex couples:** Identical.

**Implementation:** Festive or personal, e.g. *"You are the light of the world"*, *"Somewhere over the rainbow"* or a song from your life together.

A liturgical celebration of marriage does not have to be changed when two people of the same sex get married. *The form can remain the same because the content - love and the covenant before God - is the same.*

This was a complete liturgical celebration for the blessing of same-sex couples, which is based on the structure and content of classic Christian wedding ceremonies - theologically sound, inclusive and dignified.

# Biblical and spiritual arguments for the blessing of love

Critics often refer to individual biblical passages that evaluate homosexual acts (such as Lev 18:22 or Rom 1:26-27). However, many theologians point out that these texts should be read *in a historical context* and did not have the loving partnership of two people of the same sex lived today in mind. *Jesus' message of love and acceptance of all is far more central.* *"You shall love your neighbor as yourself"* - this highest commandment (Mark 12:31) makes no distinction based on gender or orientation. Jesus never explicitly opposed homosexuality; rather, he showed empathy and respect for the marginalized. He protected the adulteress from condemnation (John 8:7) and spent time with the socially ostracized. From the perspective of following Jesus, an exclusionary attitude towards LGBTQIA+ people is hardly compatible with Jesus' message.

*Jesus' central message of comprehensive love should not be restricted by selectively interpreted biblical passages* - argue many theologians today.

Positive biblical leitmotifs underpin the idea of placing loving relationships under God's blessing. The Old Testament already states: *"It is not good for man to be alone"* (Gen 2:18). Partnership and love are considered a gift from God. *"God is love, and he who abides in love abides in God, and God in him"* (1 John 4:16) - this word does not exclude sincere love from God's presence. When two people commit themselves to each other in faithfulness, care and love, Christians can recognize an image of divine love in this. *The ability to love is a divine gift*, regardless of sexual orientation.

Consequently, according to a spiritual argument, the church may not deny people who ask for a blessing for their love this sacramental blessing without acting against the essence of God - who is love.

From a spiritual and pastoral point of view, there is also much to be said for the marriage and blessing of same-sex couples. A blessing is a prayer in which the church implores God's closeness and protection for people. When two people ask for this blessing and their wedding ceremony, they are acknowledging that they *want God to work in their relationship*. The church would be fulfilling its mission to accompany these seekers. *"Where people are united in love, God is present,"* says the resolution document of the Synodal Path. A blessing at the wedding ceremony expresses that a couple wishes to *place* their relationship *within the horizon of God* and align themselves with the Gospel. It is therefore by no means a presumption to ignore God's will, but a humble prayer that God's good spirit will guide and strengthen the marriage and partnership.

# Pastoral theological perspectives: responsibility, fidelity and care

From a pastoral theological perspective, proponents of marriage ceremonies and blessings emphasize what Christian partnerships - whether hetero or homo - are essentially about: lived *responsibility, fidelity, mutual care and loving commitment.* These values are the cornerstones of every stable relationship and correspond to the Christian ethos. *Homosexual and heterosexual relationships strive for the same values and experience the same challenges: Fidelity and permanence on the one hand, possible estrangement and crises on the other.*

There are successes and failures in all partnerships. The decisive factor is that people *are committed to each other* and are prepared to stand by each other in good times and in difficult times. Where such an attitude is lived, the church recognizes something morally good, which - especially if it happens in faith - is *"worthy of blessing" at the wedding ceremony.*

The Synodal Assembly of the Catholic Church in Germany formulated this conviction clearly: *there is moral good in the life of couples who live together in commitment and mutual responsibility. Where faith comes into play, the good is worthy of blessing. The Church is blessed by the love of these couples. Such mutual love calls for blessing.*

In other words: When two people form their love carefully and responsibly - be it a heterosexual or homosexual couple - this love deserves recognition and support from the church.

It would be merciless or even discriminatory to deny such couples the blessing of the sacrament of marriage across the board.

Pastors also report that same-sex couples often ask for a church blessing during their wedding ceremony with *great earnestness.* These requests do not stem from defiance, but from a deep faith: the couples want to bring their relationship before God and pray for his support for their journey together.

The church should not see this serious longing as a threat, but as an opportunity to accompany people in their concrete lives. *"People who* ask for blessings want to experience what the church can give," explained Auxiliary Bishop Dieter Geerlings many years ago.

He emphasized that the church should not refuse to bless people who *conduct their relationship with responsibility, love and faith.*

A blessing for such couples during the wedding ceremony means asking that the relationship will succeed and that God will help. This is a deeply pastoral act of strengthening and encouragement - by no means a relativization of marriage or morality.

Ultimately, it is about *ritual accompaniment rather than judgment*. The church should not be a judge of the life plans of its faithful, but a companion. With a blessing ceremony, it can *also* emphasize *the value and dignity of non-heterosexual partnerships* and place them on an equal footing with the heterosexual sacramental blessing.

*The church is called to bless relationships, not to condemn them, and to accompany people, not to weed them out.*

This maxim, formulated in a recently published theologically inspired book, sums up the pastoral concern in a nutshell: not exclusion, but *unconditional recognition* of couples should be the guiding principle.

## Blessings in practice: Germany, Belgium and South Africa

While there has long been a lack of clarity at world church level, some local churches have already created facts - or at least driven the discourse forward. *Germany* has experienced a real awakening in recent years. Despite the Roman "no" of 2021, courageous pastors organized public blessing services across the country under the motto *"Love wins"* to set an example against discrimination. Same-sex married couples have been and continue to be blessed in many congregations.

An important impetus came from the *Synodal Path*, the reform dialog of the German church. In March 2023, the Synodal Assembly voted by a large majority in favor of *officially allowing blessings for same-sex couples*. Of the 60 German bishops, only 9 voted no - a remarkable vote in favor of change.

*Figure5 : Wedding ceremony of a queer, lesbian couple with blessing (illustration).*

*A lovingly designed, colorful illustration in a minimalist comic style that shows two happily smiling women embracing lovingly. Next to them stands a friendly, smiling figure of Jesus with a gesture of blessing, implementing the marriage ceremony of this couple, and a rainbow halo, symbolically expressing acceptance, diversity and blessing. The scene of the conferring of this sacrament conveys warmth, openness and inclusion and is particularly suitable for themes around LGBTQIA+ acceptance, same-sex love, and modern religious interpretations.*

The adopted action text *"Blessings for couples who love each other"* recommends that the Bishops' Conference *promptly develop appropriate liturgical celebrations and equate them with those for opposite-sex couples.*

In this, the Church offers recognition and support to all couples who are united in love, who treat each other with full respect and dignity and who are prepared to live their sexuality in mindfulness for themselves, for each other and in social responsibility in the long term.

Such blessings should be possible nationwide by 2026 at the latest. This vote - supported by bishops, theologians and laypeople - shows a broad conviction that blessings are pastorally *necessary* in order to remain credible as a church. Bishop Stephan Ackermann of Trier spoke of a *"theological breakthrough"* with regard to the Vatican's U-turn.

*Belgium* has also already taken bold steps. In September 2022 - i.e. before the Roman reorientation - the Flemish bishops published a document allowing blessing ceremonies for homosexual couples in Flanders.

## Objections: Is the church losing its identity?

The biggest concern of critics is: *will the Catholic Church lose its identity if it blesses homosexual couples at their wedding ceremony?* After all, it has been taught for centuries that living homosexuality is a sin and that marriage between a man and a woman is an immutable sacrament. Doesn't everything become arbitrary if same-sex partnerships are now also married in church and blessed ? These objections deserve a serious debate.

*Doctrinal identity:* The church is indeed defined by certain doctrines. This includes the understanding of marriage as a union between man and woman. *Fiducia supplicans* emphasizes that this doctrine will *not be changed.*

The identity of the church does not depend on whether it exclusively grants God's blessing to heterosexual couples. Rather, the Church's identity is rooted even more deeply in its mission to be *an instrument of love and salvation for all people.* Pope Francis often reminds us that the Church is a *"field hospital"* for the wounded - it does not lose its identity when it mercifully adapts to the real life situation of people, but rather *confirms* it.

Many are now calling for homosexual partnerships to be *married.* It is not just about a *pastoral blessing,* but about the existing sacrament of marriage.

The liturgical forms do not have to make a clear distinction.

Could God also be at work in these relationships? Theologians such as Julia Knop speak of homosexuality as a *"variant of creation",* i.e. a part of human diversity given by the Creator.

*Figure6 : Sacrament of marriage for a same-sex, gay couple by a female priest.*

*A solemn and emotional scene in a church: a priest in white liturgical robes administers the sacrament of marriage to a same-sex couple, consisting of two men in elegant suits, with her hand raised and a book in the other hand. A crucifix hangs in the background, flanked by burning candles, making the atmosphere seem spiritual and venerable. The image symbolizes the church's appreciation of the sacrament of marriage, diversity and equality as well as the acceptance of same-sex partnerships within religious communities.*

It is not a question of making all couples the same, but of doing justice to all couples. The Church would rather lose *its* identity if it only ever responded to pressing pastoral issues with prohibitions - then it would distance itself from the lives of the faithful. However, by responding creatively to new challenges, it remains *itself: a living, learning community in the spirit of God.*

# Experiences of queer Christians: "We dare and are (a) blessing"

Nothing illustrates the urgency of the issue more than the *experiences of affected believers*. In recent years, numerous Catholic *Christians* who are *lesbian, gay, bi, trans* or queer have spoken openly about their faith and their lives. Actions such as *#OutInChurch* - the coming out of 125 employees of the church in January 2022 - have shown how much these people *love the church and seek a home in it*, despite all previous rejections.

Many of them live in permanent partnerships. They are involved as church musicians, religious teachers, pastors and in community groups. Time and again, we hear the same wish from them: recognition and blessing instead of silence and taboo.

Queer Christians report that their love is *not a contradiction to their faith*, but an expression of it. A gay couple from southern Germany, for example, explained in an interview that they prayed together, organized their home as a Christian family and saw their relationship as being led by God.

The church's exclusion hurt them because it gave them the impression that their love was worth less in God's eyes. *"There is no first or second class love. There is only love,"* said Sven Lehmann, himself a devout Catholic and the German government's queer commissioner, on the occasion of the Vatican's about-turn. Many of those affected share this conviction: *love is love*, and where sincere love is lived, the church should make no distinction in its pastoral care.

Those involved report *moving moments*: A service in which they were allowed to come to the altar with their loved ones, a personal prayer from the pastor about them, perhaps an Our Father together - all of this made them feel that *they really belonged*. *"At last I feel completely accepted by my church,"* said a lesbian woman after a blessing service in Würzburg; she was now *"at peace with God and the church"* as far as her relationship was concerned (as quoted by the local press).

Such testimonies make it clear that the *spiritual dimension* of same-sex partnerships is often underestimated.

These couples live charity, forgiveness, patience and sacrifice in everyday life - all the virtues that Christian couples also strive for. Why shouldn't God's sacraments and blessings rest on them? Indeed, many say: It *has long rested on* them, because God blesses people anyway. The church's celebration of blessing makes up for what God already does in his love in a liturgical sense. It also creates visibility: queer couples do not have to hide, but are allowed to come before God as part of the congregation. This not only strengthens the couples themselves, but can also be *a testimony of reconciliation* for the congregation - reconciliation between the church and those who have long been on the margins.

For many, the best solution is ultimately *equal public treatment*: i.e. blessings and weddings as an offer for *all* couples, without a shameful special category. This  also what the #OutInChurch manifesto called for: no longer an exception, but a matter of course: full *sacramental equality* for LGBTQIA+ couples.

For the church, this means that it can learn from people how great God's love is. It is precisely by marrying these couples that it does not lose its holiness, but *finds its way back to its mission* of being a blessing for the world and creating what is good.

# Chapter 5:
# Is dogmatism spiritual truth - or the exercise of power in disguise?

*The chapter examines whether dogmatism in the Catholic Church can be understood as an authentic expression of spiritual truth or should rather be seen as a veiled exercise of power. Historically, dogmas have served to safeguard fundamental truths of faith and create unity. However, it is clear that dogmas have often been used as instruments of power to maintain authority within the church and to ward off social change. Examples of this are the dogma of papal infallibility, which is often thematized as a centralist concentration of power, and the strict Catholic sexual morality, which often comes into conflict with the reality of the lives of the faithful and serves as an instrument of social control. The claim to absoluteness ("Extra ecclesiam nulla salus") is also questioned, as it makes interreligious dialog more difficult and ignores the diversity of spiritual experiences. A reflective and dialogical theology can emerge that questions dogmatic teachings and creates space for personal decisions of conscience in order to prevent the church from becoming rigid.*

- *Question: How can the Catholic Church reform dogmas so that they once again become viable, dynamic points of reference for faith instead of remaining rigid instruments for exercising power?*
- *Question: Isn't it an expression of spiritual arrogance when a church claims to possess immutable truths while ignoring the reality of life and the decisions of conscience of its believers?*
- *Option for action: The Catholic Church should initiate a binding, global synodal process in which problematic dogmas such as papal infallibility, sexual morality and the claim to absoluteness are reflexively questioned and reformed in line with today's theological and social insights.*

- **Training option:** Clergy, believers and students in religious education should develop skills for questioning reflection, conscience formation and interreligious and intercultural dialog competence, for example through workshops and seminars on theological hermeneutics, ethics and modern anthropological findings, in order to credibly exemplify a reflective, open and realistic understanding of dogmas.

In Christian history, the term *dogma* stands for an irrefutable doctrine. The Greek *dógma* literally means "opinion, doctrine". A dogma is more than a mere personal opinion: it is a *fixed definition of a truth of faith* that is proclaimed as absolutely true by the ecclesiastical authority. According to the Catholic understanding, dogmas are even *"truths revealed by God and solemnly defined by the Magisterium"* - i.e. doctrines of the highest order to which all believers should adhere. Although a *theological doctrine* encompasses all church beliefs, it can develop further as long as it does not contradict the dogma.

Finally, theological opinions are individual views of theologians which (for the time being) have no binding status and therefore make no claim to absolute truth.

*Dogmas* therefore claim to be binding and unchangeable, whereas doctrines can also contain time-related views and opinions of a purely personal nature.

## Development of dogmas: guardians of truth and risk of absolutization

Dogmas arose primarily to clarify and preserve central truths of faith. In *the early church*, fundamental dogmas were formulated in councils - for example on the *Trinity* (God's triune nature) and the *divinity of Christ* - in order to safeguard the unity of faith against internal contradictions.

Such dogmas had a legitimate function: they were intended to define the foundation of the Christian faith and protect it from falsification. In 325, for example, the Council of Nicaea made it clear that Christ *was "of one essence with the Father"* in order to resolve the controversy surrounding Jesus' nature. In this sense, dogmas acted as *guardians of the truth of the faith* and gave the faithful guidance.

However, the list of binding doctrines also grew over time - and with it the danger of elevating relative theological views to *absolute ones*. Each era tended to dogmatize certain understandings of faith.

For example, it was not until *1854* that Pope Pius IX defined the dogma of the *Immaculate Conception of Mary* and *in 1870* that the First Vatican Council defined *papal infallibility*. Such late dogmas arose partly as a defensive reaction against the spirit of the times (such as the proclamation of papal infallibility in the midst of a church struggle in the modern age). By *dogmatizing*, the church tries to withstand challenges, but runs the risk of hardening itself in the process.

Dogmatism - the rigid adherence to dogmas - often serves institutionally as a protective mechanism against change.

By defining certain teachings as unquestionable truths, the church preserves its authority and the continuity of tradition, *but at the same time makes it difficult for itself to react to new social developments or scientific findings.*

History shows that such a defensive stance can create tensions: For example, when the discovery of the heliocentric view of the world called the biblically based geocentric cosmos into question, *the church initially reacted by condemning it as "false doctrine".* Conflicts arose time and again when new insights collided with existing dogmas. This shows the dilemma: *dogmas can clarify faith and create identity, but their claim to absoluteness carries the risk of blocking further development.*

# Criticism of dogmatism: when faith becomes rigid and marginalizing

Dogmatism in the religious sense means not only the existence of dogmas, but also an attitude of rigid unwaveringness. Colloquially speaking, "dogmatists" also have an intolerant connotation - someone who insists unwaveringly on their point of view and does not tolerate any contradiction.

This mindset becomes problematic when rules of faith become more important than faith itself. Rigid adherence can lead to spiritual *numbness*: Religion is then lived as an unchanging system of rules instead of a living path to God.

*Figure7 : Dogmatism as an instrument of power.*

*A stimulating illustration in the style of a vintage poster that symbolically and artistically depicts control and manipulation by church authority. On the left is a serious and authoritarian-looking bishop raising his finger in a warning gesture and holding a book with a cross. To the right is a sad and resigned-looking man who is controlled like a marionette by large red hands on invisible strings. The color scheme is reduced and rich in contrast, with dark, muted tones, which underlines the dramatic character of the picture. This depiction illustrates the themes of abuse of power, dogmatism, questions to authority figures and freedom of the individual within religious communities.*

Dogmatism tends not to allow any dissenting opinions. When a doctrine is considered infallible and definitive, there is often little room for questions or new perspectives. *Dissenters* - be they reform-minded theologians or simply believers with a conscience - run the risk of being ostracized. Dogmatic systems clearly define what is to be considered truth and are quick to label deviations as error or sin. This can create an atmosphere in which open discussion is suppressed. As a result, reflective questions are not asked and individual decisions of conscience are not respected. In one lecture it was pointedly stated: *Dogmatic thinking demands submission to a foreign authority* - you believe something "not because you understand it, but solely on the basis of someone else's insight."

Such a belief out of pure obedience restricts personal spiritual development and can plunge people into conflicts of loyalty when their own conscience or reason comes to different conclusions.

In addition, dogmatism can develop an intolerant dynamic. *Dogmatism ... promotes intolerance and violence when it claims to be the only truth and categorizes deviations as threatening or sinful*, as was already pointed out in the first volume of *Deus Ex Machina (Part I: On the Questioning Life)*.

Those who believe they are in sole possession of the absolute truth tend to devalue other views as error. This can easily lead to a rejection of other perspectives and even fear of anything that does not fit into one's own scheme of things.

*History shows* that dogmatic convictions have been used time and again to exclude or suppress those who think differently. Think of the Inquisition and the persecution of heretics, religious wars or the condemnation of entire groups on the basis of deviant lifestyles. If a religious system does not tolerate diversity, the claim to truth can quickly turn into discrimination or coercion.

A dogmatic approach is particularly problematic when it comes to ethical issues because it blocks social change. Changes in moral concepts - for example with regard to gender equality or acceptance of different sexual orientations - are then strictly resisted and existing injustices may be *religiously legitimized*. For example, discrimination against LGBTQIA+ people or the subordination of women could be justified for centuries with supposed divine authority.

A rigid adherence to outdated doctrines "sanctified" social imbalances and made corrections more difficult.

*The price* of dogmatism can be an inner ossification of the church: Rules of faith are formally upheld, but many people become inwardly alienated. Quite a few ask themselves whether such a belief in immutable rules still has anything to do with their lives. Spiritually speaking, a religion that only insists on dogma and obedience is in danger of losing its liberating core. Where dogmas become more important than the individual, faith freezes into a religion of laws.

More recent awakenings show that things can be done differently: an open, reflective spirituality emphasizes dialogue, mercy and reason rather than absolute truths. Many believers today - including theologians and even bishops - want a church that leaves room for personal decisions of conscience and theological debates.

Many Catholics therefore welcome the fact that the Pope has *not* proclaimed *any new infallible dogmas* for decades - because this gives the faithful more freedom to contribute their own insights and make decisions based on their conscience.

Dogmas therefore do not necessarily have to act as "spiritual shackles". If they are handled with humility and questioned in the light of new insights, faith can remain alive. Otherwise, dogmatism actually threatens to degenerate into *"spiritual control in Sunday garb"* - as it was once thought-provokingly put - in other words, into an exercise of power that hides behind sacred concepts.

# Today's dogmas put to the test: examples and need for reform

In view of this problem, reflexive questions today focus on certain church dogmas and doctrines that are considered to be in need of reform. Four examples stand out:

### 1. Virgin birth of Mary - biological miracle or symbolic testimony of faith?

**The dogma:** The doctrine of the virgin birth states that Mary conceived Jesus *without* the involvement of a man. Jesus was conceived in her womb by the Holy Spirit - Mary remained a *"perpetual virgin"*. This statement can already be found in the early church creeds and is based on the biblical Christmas narratives (Mt 1:18 and Lk 1:34f.). It was defined by the Church around the 4th century in the context of Christology: Jesus' unique divine origin was to be emphasized.

**Historical context:** In ancient times, miraculous births were not unknown in religious tales - think of heroic legends in which gods impregnate human mothers. Christian dogma was understood as a *mystery of faith* that emphasized Jesus' sonship with God. For a long time, it was hardly questioned literally by the church. It was only in modern times, with a growing scientific understanding of biology, that the literal understanding of the virgin birth came under scrutiny. Theologians such as Uta Ranke-Heinemann began to reflect on this doctrine. Ranke-Heinemann, the world's first habilitated Catholic theologian, openly doubted the biological reality of the virgin birth - and lost her church teaching license in 1987 as a result.

She argued that the idea of Mary's perpetual virginity was less a historical account than a theological construction that imposed an unrealistic ideal of purity on women and served to control female sexuality. Instead of conveying a *liberating* message for the faithful, this dogma ultimately contributed to the sexual morality of the church, which suppressed women and their physicality.

**Points of criticism:** From a *biological* point of view, a human virgin birth - natural *parthenogenesis* - is extremely unlikely to impossible. Even if an egg cell were to divide without fertilization, only female offspring could be produced by chance, as the male chromosome set is missing.

The modern natural sciences therefore *do not* regard dogma as a biological fact, but as a religious concept outside the realm of scientific possibilities.

Historically, Bible scholars point out that the Old Testament scripture on which the virgin birth is based (Isaiah 7:14) only speaks of a "young woman" in the original Hebrew text; only the Greek translation (Septuagint) turned it into *"parthénos"*, i.e. *virgin*. It is therefore possible that the Church's literal interpretation is based on a translation accent or error that was not originally intended.

Critics complain that the Church is clinging to a biologically improbable assertion here, which inevitably brings it into conflict with modern reason. Pastorally, too, it is questionable what the fixation on Mary's physical integrity achieves: Does this not implicitly view sexuality as a flaw? Aren't believers being led into an unnecessary ordeal between faith and reason? In short: the dogma, understood literally, is caught between *faith and biological reality*.

**Alternative perspectives:** Many theologians today argue in favor of interpreting the virgin birth symbolically. The *intention of the statement* is important: God himself is the origin of Jesus - *this* can also be believed without thinking of a gynecological process. In this sense, the virgin birth could be understood as a linguistic image to express the unique closeness of God in Jesus. Modern exegetes emphasize this: The decisive factor is that God became man in Jesus - *how* exactly is beyond scientific proof. In fact, the dogma is still an integral part of the *creed*, for example, but even many clergy are open to a demythologizing interpretation. The core theological message - Jesus' divine mission - can be preserved *without* adhering to the biological understanding of antiquity. In this way, a bridge can be built: The virgin birth would then no longer be a "medical fact" to be defended, but a symbol of faith for God's miraculous action. This would take the pressure off the question and the dogma would lose its shadow of power.

## 2. Infallibility of the Pope - truth of faith or instrument of power?

**The dogma:** *Papal infallibility* is a relatively young dogma. It was defined by the First Vatican Council in 1870 and states that whenever the Pope, as the supreme shepherd of the Church, proclaims a final decision ex cathedra (i.e. with the highest teaching authority) in matters of faith or morals, he is infallible - his statement is then considered to be free of error and binding for all Catholics.

It is important to note that this privilege only applies to very specific solemn doctrinal decisions (by no means to *every* utterance of the Pope) and has been used extremely rarely in history - for example in the case of the dogmas of the Immaculate Conception (1854) and the Assumption of Mary (1950).

The dogma of infallibility originally served to emphasize the supreme teaching authority of the Pope and to safeguard the unity of doctrine against the rise of *modernism* and national church tendencies.

**Historical context:** The proclamation of papal infallibility came at a time when the Catholic Church was under political and cultural pressure (keyword: *Kulturkampf*). By defining this doctrinal authority, Rome tightened the reins: a bulwark was created against the spread of liberal theologies and the papacy was strengthened in a centralized manner. However, the dogma was already controversial at the time - a minority of the Council Fathers rejected it, and some theologians broke away from Rome (*Old Catholics*). In the decades that followed, this instrument was only used very cautiously, knowing full well that every infallible decision is practically irreformable.

**Points of criticism:** Especially today, infallibility is often perceived *as the epitome of the church's exercise of power.* Concentration of authority on one person - so the accusation - contradicts the biblical principle of the community of all believers. The famous theologian Hans Küng openly questioned whether a person (even a pope) could really be absolutely free of error in matters of faith and argued that this doctrine could not be clearly proven biblically, but was a later ecclesiastical power construct.

Instead, Hans Küng called for a church that relied less on hierarchical authority and more on the original spirit of the Gospel. This questioning of papal infallibility brought him into deep conflict with the Vatican at the time and led to the withdrawal of his teaching license in 1979 - a clear sign of how *sensitive* the issue of earning money within the church system still is today - but Hans Küng continued to publish despite the withdrawal of his economic basis.

Critics also see the dogma of infallibility as an exaggeration of the papal office, which makes reforms more difficult: after all, how can you correct obvious mistakes if you have previously claimed that the supreme leader cannot be wrong? There is a great temptation to deny mistakes so as not to undermine the principle of infallibility. For example, church historians accuse Pope Paul VI of upholding the ban on artificial contraception (*encyclical Humanae Vitae*) in 1968 against the advice of many experts - less out of theological conviction than out of fear of undermining the authority of earlier doctrinal decisions.

Infallibility can thus become a blockade: Even if a later pope were aware that a dogma causes pastoral problems, the official correction would appear to be a serious loss of face. The exercise of power here therefore consists of insisting on one's own claim to absoluteness - even at the cost of loss of credibility or stagnation.

**Possible alternatives:** Based on these difficulties, there is a growing number of voices that want to *relativize* or reinterpret the dogma of infallibility. One approach is to emphasize the infallibility of the faith community rather than the infallibility of a single person. For example, the infallible proclamation by the Pope could be replaced by a communal theological reflection process in which the Holy Spirit guides the Church as a whole through dialog - for example at councils or synods.

In fact, Catholic ecclesiology also recognizes the concept of the *infallibility of the Church as a whole* in matters concerning the sense of faith of all believers (*sensus fidei*). In practice, this would mean that it is not an isolated pronouncement "from above" that is considered definitive, but a broad consensus that emerges through prayer and discussion. Some theologians suggest that the dogma should be classified historically: It was a *response to the needs of the 19th century* - but different answers may be needed today. A disempowered infallibility would also mean admitting errors where they have occurred. Hans Küng once outlined the vision that a pope would have to have the courage to *say: "I was wrong"* - for example on the issue of how to deal with women, homosexuals or the claim to power.

For a long time, this sounded utopian. But interestingly, Pope Francis actually said: *"I was wrong"* - in an interview in 2014, he admitted to making personal mistakes. This signals a change: away from the aura of never being able to be wrong and towards a culture of recognizing mistakes. In the future, the Church could handle infallibility in such a way that it only protects the core of the faith (for example: God is love), *but does not* fix *every doctrinal issue* in absolute terms. This would essentially preserve unity without blocking necessary reforms. Ultimately, it is about decentralizing the search for truth: Not just the Pope alone, but the whole Church listening to one another would become the guardian of truth.

## 3 "Extra ecclesiam nulla salus" - The Church's claim to absoluteness and interreligious dialog

**The dogma:** *"Outside the church there is no salvation"* - this sentence from the old church doctrine sums up the claim to exclusivity that Christianity (and the Catholic Church in particular) has long made. In essence, it means that one's own religion - in this case belonging to the Catholic Church - is the only way to salvation; other faiths ultimately do not lead to the goal.

This exclusive claim was upheld for centuries and shaped mission and theology: the church saw itself as *the only true guardian of divine truth*. Other religions were either regarded as erroneous or at best as imperfect approximations of the truth. This was dogmatically enshrined at the Council of Florence (1442), for example, which unequivocally taught that no one outside the Catholic Church could be saved.

**Historical development:** The Second Vatican Council (1962-65) marked a turning point. In the declaration *Nostra Aetate* (1965) and in the decree *Lumen Gentium*, traditional exclusivism was significantly softened. Since then, the Catholic Church has not rejected anything that is "true and holy" in other religions and recognizes that in them *"there is not infrequently found a ray of that truth which enlightens all men."*

Nevertheless, the Council held that the fullness of salvation is given in Christ and therefore in the Church founded by him. There was thus a change to an attitude of "open exclusivism": other religions may have parts of the truth, but ultimately *only Christ* (and, according to Catholic understanding, the connection to his Church) leads to final salvation. This more inclusive language was a big step towards the rest of the world - not least in relation to Judaism and the world religions. The Church now sought dialog instead of confrontation, which theologically meant a certain relativization of its claim to absoluteness, without giving it up completely.

**Points of criticism:** Despite the opening up brought about by Vatican II, a tension remains. Critics complain that the Catholic Church *de facto* still clings to a claim to absoluteness - albeit in a more polite form. The statement that in Christ lies the fullness of truth and salvation implies that other paths are necessarily deficient. In a pluralistic world in which billions of people belong to other religions, this quickly comes across as presumptuous. Representatives of other faith communities sometimes perceive the claim that only the Christian faith leads to the ultimate truth as an affront. Subtle exclusivism can also make *interfaith dialog* more difficult: If participation in the conversation is premised from the outset on one of the partners possessing "the complete truth", genuine encounters at eye level become difficult. The theological objection is that such an exclusive claim does not do justice either to the mystery of

God - who can also show himself to others according to his own counsel - or to the complexity of religious experiences. After all, there are also deep spiritual truths and paths to salvation in other religions, which many believers acknowledge today.

**Approaches and alternatives:** In theology, inclusivism and pluralism have developed as a counter-model. Inclusivism means that although Christ is the Savior of all, his grace also works *invisibly* in other religions - their followers can therefore be saved, even without formal church membership. Pluralism goes one step further and places different religions side by side on an equal footing as different paths to one divine goal. The Catholic Church has so far rejected complete pluralism because, in its view, it jeopardizes the uniqueness of Christ. But there is movement internally: Theologians such as Jacques Dupuis and Paul Knitter have argued for a much greater appreciation of God's work in the diversity of religions. In his dialogue with Islam and other religions, Pope Francis repeatedly emphasizes the brotherhood of all people under one God. In 2019, for example, Francis signed a document with a Grand Imam in Abu Dhabi that describes the *diversity of religions as intended by God* - a remarkable step towards a humble recognition of religious diversity.

One possible reform for the church is to further relativize its remaining claim to exclusivity without giving up its core faith. In concrete terms, this could mean that the church continues to see itself as a community commissioned by Christ, *but renounces its implicit or explicit claim to be the sole institution of salvation*. Instead, it would see itself as one of several ways in which people find God - convinced of its truth, but open to the fact that God is not limited to the visible boundaries of the church. Such an attitude promotes genuine dialog, because people treat each other with mutual respect. Basically, this would be a return to Jesus' words that the Spirit *"blows where he wills"* (John 3:8). *Humility* instead of triumphalism could be the motto. In many regions, the church of the 21st century has long been one of many players in the religious field. Its mission to bear witness to Christ remains - but it can do so without claiming power, in a cooperative spirit. This would turn dogmatic exclusivity into an inclusive, open church that has its own identity but seriously respects others in their different relationship with God.

## 4. Rigid sexual morality - challenges for conscience and lived love

**The "dogma":** Strictly speaking, sexual morality is not a single dogma, but a series of binding doctrinal judgments of the Church. Nevertheless, certain moral-theological doctrines are treated by the church hierarchy as de facto dogmas - as immutable truths. These include: *Sexuality* belongs exclusively within the marriage of a man and a woman; every sexual act must remain *open* to procreation (hence the ban on artificial contraception); homosexuality is rejected as "intrinsically disordered"; sex before or outside of marriage is considered a grave sin. These moral norms have been taught for centuries and explicitly affirmed by popes such as Paul VI (Encyclical *Humanae Vitae*, 1968) and John Paul II. They are based on a traditional, naturalistic view: God intended sexuality primarily for procreation, therefore its legitimate practice is limited to conjugal love with the intention of procreation. For decades, this was the official line - deviations were hardly tolerated.

**Problems and points of criticism:** Nowadays, these guidelines meet with widespread rejection, even within the church. From a medical and scientific point of view, sexuality is a basic human need that fulfills a variety of functions - bonding, pleasure, communication - not just reproduction. From a biological point of view, the strict link between the sexual act and procreation appears artificial: people also practice sexuality outside of fertile phases and often deliberately without the desire to have children. The church's moral teachings ignored such facts for a long time and held on to an ideal that fails to reflect the lived reality of many. In terms of social ethics, the church's sexual morals are said to be *distant from life* and burden the faithful with feelings of guilt. In fact, the preaching was often characterized by negative rhetoric: sex outside the norm was portrayed as a sin, a flaw, even a danger. Theologian Ranke-Heinemann, for example, accused the church of creating *fear and guilt* with its sexual teachings, instead of promoting a life-affirming view of the body and love.

Many Catholics could not and would not abide by these rules - and either felt like bad Christians or turned away in disappointment. A widely known fact: the vast majority of self-practicing Catholics use contraception and live sexuality on their own responsibility, regardless of the prohibition. This discrepancy between the doctrinal ideal and actual practice has severely damaged the authority of the Church.

The aspect of power control through sexual norms is also addressed. Historically, the church's strict sexual morals allowed it to control the private lives of the faithful. For example, by making contraception sinful and severely punishing adultery, the church exerted influence over people's most intimate decisions. Women were particularly affected by this: They were deprived of the freedom to make decisions about their reproduction, which forced them into traditional roles.

In many Catholic countries (e.g. Ireland in the past, Poland or Latin America), church regulations led to contraceptives or abortion being banned or severely restricted by law - with sometimes serious consequences for women's health and self-determination,

Here, dogmatism shows itself in its power-political dimension: a moral doctrine was used to exert social control, often without regard for individual suffering.

**Reform and change:** In recent decades, a rethink has been initiated by theologians, lay associations and even some bishops. More and more church people are calling for a further development of sexual ethics in the light of today's human scientific findings and the reality of life for believers. The German *Synodal Way*, for example, has spoken out by a large majority in favour of a "modernization of the church's sexual morality", including a reassessment of contraception and homosexuality in the catechism.

One of the adopted texts even states that same-sex love is *not a sin* and that homosexual orientation is part of a person's identity as intended by God - words that recently seemed unthinkable in the official church. Such topics were also openly discussed at a global church level, for example at the 2023 World Synod of Bishops. Although there is still resistance from a conservative wing (some of the bishops temporarily blocked a reform paper on sexual morality in 2022), the trend is clearly moving in the direction of change.

**Future perspective:** A renewed Catholic sexual morality would place love, responsibility and conscience at the center. Sexuality would not primarily be seen as a danger zone that needs to be regulated, but as a *gift from God* that should be shaped with care and love. This includes reliability and mutual respect - but without blanket exclusion of certain lifestyles. For example, contraception could be recognized as responsible family planning if it is done for good reasons and the couple can justify it before God. Homosexual couples could be treated with appreciation and their love recognized as valuable instead of condemning them to celibacy. Young people could be accompanied sexually without condemning them for every misstep. In short, the church could switch from a system of commandments to an ethic of accompaniment and empowerment. Some steps in this direction are already visible - for example, when individual bishops advocate blessing ceremonies with a sacramental character for same-sex couples or Pope Francis emphasizes that no one should be excluded from the church because of their sexual orientation. However, a definitive change of course is still pending. However, it would be necessary in order to bridge the gap between dogma and life and restore the credibility of the church, especially among young people.

## New beginnings instead of stagnation: Synodal paths and freedom of conscience

The examples show: The tension between spiritual truth and the exercise of power in dogma is not an abstract, but a highly concrete challenge of today. But how can the church deal with it? A look at current reform processes offers clues. In Germany, the aforementioned Synodal Path (2019-2023) has shown that many believers and pastors are willing to openly address even sensitive topics - from dealing with power in the church to sexual morality and women's issues. A synodal world process has been underway internationally since 2021, in which bishops *and* laypeople are discussing the future of the church together. This *World Synod of Bishops* in Rome, the first phase of which took place in 2023, has also made it clear that questions are being asked about participation, gender equality and a new approach to diversity. Although concrete resolutions are still tentative, the culture of listening and dialog alone marks a change from previous dogmatic top-down thinking.

In order to rethink dogmas that are recognized today as being in need of reform, a structured process of ecclesial reflection is needed. One possible approach would be to convene an *official forum* - such as a world synod of bishops or even a council - that explicitly deals with controversial doctrinal issues. It would be important to work on an interdisciplinary basis: Theology, human sciences (psychology, sociology, medicine) and the experiences of the faithful should come into conversation. Only in this way can a holistic view emerge. Freedom of conscience is also central: the Church should recognize that the Holy Spirit speaks not only through magisterial definitions, but also in the *forum internum* of individual believers. What people recognize in honest conscience before God - e.g. that the use of contraception is their responsibility, or that their homosexual love is accepted by God - must no longer be dismissed wholesale as error. A renewed relationship between doctrinal authority and conscience would mean that dogmatic teachings would always seek to be tied back to the lived reality of believers.

It would be conceivable, for example, to convene regional synods to draw up concrete reform proposals (similar to the Synodal Path) and then bundle these together for the global church. Such a process would have to be transparent and dialogical in order to build trust. The participation of women and marginalized groups would be crucial so that the existing power hierarchy does not just confirm itself. Experienced theologians - including those who have been criticized in the past (such as Hans Küng or Uta Ranke-Heinemann) - could also be rehabilitated posthumously and their ideas acknowledged in order to show that they are being heard: *Criticism is heard.* After all, the Church should not be afraid to admit mistakes. In the Jubilee Year 2000, John Paul II asked for forgiveness for the Church's errors (Crusades, persecution of the Jews, etc.) - a historic act. With similar openness, we could say today that *in some dogmas we have confused human limitations with divine truth.* That would not be a betrayal of faith, but a sign of greatness and truthfulness.

The willingness to rethink old dogmas does not mean giving up everything. It is a matter of *discerning* what is really the truth of faith and what is a temporary shell. This process requires courage - the courage to change in faithfulness. Pope Francis often speaks of a "*synodality*" of the Church, in which everyone is on a journey together and learns from each other. The end result may not be the abolition of all controversial dogmas, but a *deepening* or *re-evaluation* that allows God's message to shine more credibly.

Such a change is aimed at renewing the church from within. Artificial intelligence, the *deus ex machina,* often formulates a vision of a church in a variety of contexts that is based on love rather than control, that thinks rather than forbids, that opens up - and a faith that liberates rather than shames (see also Volume I).

In this spirit, dogmatism would no longer be an instrument of domination, but would be transformed into a *questioning theology that is willing to learn.* The *truth of* the Gospel would remain the guiding principle - but a living truth characterized by love, not a rigid doctrine. In this way, new spiritual vitality could grow out of today's torpor. Dogmas would then have their proper function: not as a power dictate "from above", but as shared landmarks of faith that are repeatedly tested and aligned with the word of God and the lives of people. This would hopefully make the question posed at the beginning superfluous - because spiritual truth and church action would then no longer be a contradiction in terms, but would together bear witness to the liberating message of Christ.

# Chapter 6:
# Does sexuality have to be tied to procreation - or can it also be an expression of pleasure and relationship?

The chapter deals with Catholic doctrine, which traditionally links sexuality closely to procreation. Historically influenced by theologians such as Augustine and Thomas Aquinas, the Church considers sexual acts that are not aimed at procreation to be morally questionable. The encyclical "Humanae Vitae" by Pope Paul VI in particular reinforced this view in 1968 by rejecting artificial contraceptives. This traditional sexual ethic is perceived as distant from life and alienating, as it does not correspond to the psychological or social reality of many people. Modern views see sexuality as an expression of lust, love, identity and emotional attachment, which is also confirmed in the Bible, particularly in the Song of Songs. Theologically, the view that sexuality is a gift from God that goes far beyond biological reproduction and should also be understood as a spiritual dimension of human relationships is increasingly gaining ground.

- **Question:** How can the Catholic Church reform its sexual ethics so that it sees sexuality not just as an instrument of reproduction, but recognizes it as a positive, holistic gift from God?
- **Question:** Is it not an expression of theological and pastoral irresponsibility if the Church continues to advocate a sexual ethic that primarily places lust and love under suspicion and thus morally discredits the life and identity of many believers?
- **Option for action:** The Catholic Church should break the close link between sexuality and procreation and establish an integrative sexual ethic that values sexuality as an expression of

*love, pleasure and relationship and emphasizes responsibility, mutual respect and dignity.*

- **Training option:** *Clergy, believers and students in religious education should be trained in sex education, emotional intelligence and diversity-sensitive theological ethics, for example through workshops and seminars that bring together biblical, psychological and sociological perspectives on sexuality in order to be able to credibly represent a responsible, holistic and life-affirming attitude.*

The Catholic Church is still considered by many to be hostile to sex and pleasure. Historically, it has *"long rejected mutual enjoyment of the body"* - even if cautious adjustments have been made in more recent times.

However, these traditional shadows still linger. At a time when modern societies view sexuality as part of love, identity and joie de vivre, the question arises anew: does sexuality necessarily have to be geared towards procreation - or can it also be seen as an expression of pleasure and relationship? In the following, the magisterial position of the Church and its theological roots are examined, points of criticism and human experiences are highlighted and new perspectives on inclusive sexual ethics are discussed.

## Church teaching: Marriage, procreation and sexual morality

For a long time, Catholic doctrine defined sexuality almost exclusively in the context of marriage and offspring. According to this, sexuality is only morally permitted within sacramental marriage and is bound to openness for the procreation of children. Every marital act had to remain *open* to procreation; it was not enough to simply be generally prepared to become parents.

This view shaped the church's self-image for centuries.

The church father Augustine (354-430) already emphasized that sexual pleasure in itself is sinful, unless the sexual act specifically serves the procreation of offspring. According to Augustine's drastic statement, anything else - sexuality for mere pleasure - degraded the wife to a "harlot".

The scholastic tradition also taught in this spirit: in the 13th century, Thomas Aquinas developed a sexual morality *based on natural law*, according to which the natural purpose of sexuality is procreation. All sexual acts that thwart this primary purpose (such as contraception, masturbation or same-sex sex) were considered "unnatural" and therefore sinful.

It was only in the modern era that a hesitant rethink began. The Second Vatican Council (1962-65) emphasized that marital sexuality was not only for procreation, but also for the loving bond between the partners and their happiness.

*Figure8 : Before a tender touch ...*

*A classic, Renaissance-style painting of two angels sitting opposite each other and gently moving their index fingers towards each other - an allusion to Michelangelo's famous Creation scene from the Sistine Chapel. The angels wear flowing robes in delicate, muted colors. Their faces are calm and concentrated, creating an atmosphere of spiritual connection and harmony. The background is simple and shows fine, antique cracks that emphasize the historical flair of the artwork. This depiction is ideal for themes around spiritual connection, communication, divine inspiration, harmony and first tender experience.*

In the official language of the church, love and the *"welfare of the spouses"* were now recognized as equally important purposes of marriage alongside procreation.

However, Pope Paul VI expressly confirmed the traditional line in the 1968 encyclical *Humanae Vitae*: *"Every single sexual act"* must remain open to new life. He rejected artificial contraceptives, but allowed natural conception (calendar method).

This stance - later vehemently defended by John Paul II - cemented the magisterial link between sexuality and procreation to this day.

# Theological roots: natural law, Aquinas and *Humanae Vitae*

The link between sexuality and procreation has deep theological roots in church doctrine. According to the classical doctrine of natural law - decisively influenced by Thomas Aquinas - it is in line with the God-given natural order that sexual intercourse is ordered towards procreation. The creation mandate *"Be fruitful and multiply"* (Genesis 1:28) was understood as a divine purpose. *Humanae Vitae* quoted this natural law thinking and formulated the inseparability of the unitive aspect and the procreative aspect of marital acts. To this day, the Catechism speaks of an *"indissoluble link between sexuality and procreation"* - a premise that is hardly substantiated any further.

Reflective theologians therefore ask persistently: *Why should procreation be the decisive yardstick for the moral evaluation of a sexual act, regardless of whether it is done in love and responsibility?*

Looking at tradition, it becomes clear that cultural contexts helped to shape sexual ethics. Augustine's strict condemnation of lust was also influenced by his earlier Manichaeism, which regarded everything physical as low.

The scholasticism of the Middle Ages also hardly knew any positive words for lust - sexuality was primarily defined in functional terms. This view was incorporated into the development of church doctrine over the centuries. Even in the 20th century, the Church struggled with this question: during the Council, many theologians called for an opening in the way contraception was dealt with, but Paul VI decided against any change - also out of concern for the authority of the Magisterium.

The line taken was theologically conservative: it was based on earlier magisterial statements and principles of natural law, which regarded a change in sexual morality as a danger to the divine order.

# Criticism: Functional sexual morality and alienation from life

The purely functional interpretation of sexuality sparked increasing criticism in the 20th century - even within the church. Many felt that traditional sexual morals were unrealistic and "alien to life".

When Pope Paul VI prevented any liberalization in 1968, even Catholic theologians described the official doctrine as *"rigid, ahistorical and alien to life"*.

This judgment sums up what is still criticized today: A morality that evaluates sexuality almost exclusively according to its reproductive benefits misses the point of lived human experience.

In fact, most married couples - and most people in general - have a much more holistic approach to sexuality. Lovers do not experience being desired as degradation, but as a sign of being beautiful and valuable, observes moral theologian Martin Lintner.

Lived experiences thus directly contradict the old fear (since Augustine) that lust turns the other person into an object. On the contrary: today, mutual lust is understood as an expression of appreciation and loving attraction.

Many pastors report that the strict fixation on reproduction ignores reality and often creates more feelings of guilt than meaning in life. For example, Uta Ranke-Heinemann, a renowned Catholic theologian and critic of the church, says that the absolute ban on artificial contraception is an *"unrealistic paternalism"* that robs women of their self-determination and forces them into outdated roles. The Church's teaching, which rejects *all* forms of artificial contraception, contradicts couples' responsibility for sensible family planning.

Uta Ranke-Heinemann therefore called for a reform that grants women more autonomy and no longer links sexuality exclusively with reproduction.

Her criticism sums up a widespread sentiment: a sexual morality that only allows lust and tenderness as a means to an end has an alienating effect. It ignores the human wholeness created by God, which includes body and soul, procreation *and* love.

## More than procreation: sexuality as love, lust and relationship

Regardless of dogma, a look at psychology and sexology shows that sexuality fulfills *many* functions. Sexuality does not necessarily have to be tied to reproduction - it has numerous dimensions that go beyond biological reproduction, such as intimacy, love, bonding and pleasure.

Modern studies show that a fulfilling sex life contributes significantly to mental well-being: sexuality promotes trust, closeness and emotional security between partners.

These aspects are completely independent of whether a couple can or wants to have children.

In fact, there are countless realities of life in which sexuality does not serve the purpose of procreation - for example in married couples who are unintentionally childless, in same-sex couples or in people who consciously decide against having (more) children.

To deny them all that their sexuality can be meaningful and valuable would not do justice to the lived reality.

The Bible itself does not only deal with sexuality in the context of procreation. One impressive example is the Song of Songs in the Old Testament - a collection of poetic love songs that celebrate erotic love *without* any mention of procreation.

This unabashed celebration of physical love *("With the kisses of his mouth he covers me; sweeter than wine is your love..."* - Song of Solomon 1:2) has long been spiritualized allegorically, but read literally it shows that physical lust and passion have their place in the Holy Scriptures. Today, many Christians are convinced that sexuality is not something dark or bad, but a wonderful gift from God, as theologian Karl Veitschegger puts it.

They rightly refer to the Scriptures - the Song of Songs - and to the experience that God created man as a sexual being.

Modern Catholic theology has partially integrated this insight. Pope Benedict XVI (Joseph Ratzinger) already spoke of the historical hostility towards the body as a *"particularly tragic and dark chapter in Christian thought"*.

Pope Francis has recently gone one step further: in his letter *Amoris laetitia* (2016), there is *no* longer any devaluation of lust . On the contrary, Francis emphasizes the positive significance of passion: *"Desires, feelings, emotions - what the classics called 'passions' - have an important place in marriage,"* he writes (AL 143).

And further: *"Sexuality [is] also experienced as a participation in the fullness of life in Christ's resurrection"* (AL 317).

In other words, sexuality, pleasure and even physical pleasure can have a *spiritual* dimension from a Christian perspective - as part of life in God. These statements mark a clear change from earlier doctrines.

## Spiritual dimension beyond reproduction

In addition to the psychological and social aspects, the spiritual dimension of sexuality is increasingly gaining ground - *beyond* the pure procreative perspective. Many theologians today are asking: *can sexual union not also be an expression of God's selfless love, a foretaste of divine joy?* After all, the Church understands marriage as a reflection of the covenant between Christ and the Church. But if marriage is more than a reproductive union, then sexuality within this relationship must also be allowed to be more than a reproductive act.

In fact, sexuality has always been used as a metaphor for the relationship with God in Christian mysticism - think of the intimate descriptions in the Song of Songs or the ecstatic language of some saints. A purely biological view would not do justice to the *sacrament of marriage*: in conjugal love, the physical and the sacred come together. Anyone who has ever felt the deep security of a loving embrace or the unity of two lovers may sense something transcendent in this. As one commentator writes: "In sexuality, deep gratitude towards God, deep love for your partner and healthy love for yourself can manifest themselves.

This insight emphasizes that sexuality can also be interpreted spiritually - as a *gift* in which the joy of God's creation shines through.

*Figure9 : A rainbow banner in front of a church - a symbol of diversity and the demand for queer love to be recognized in the church.*

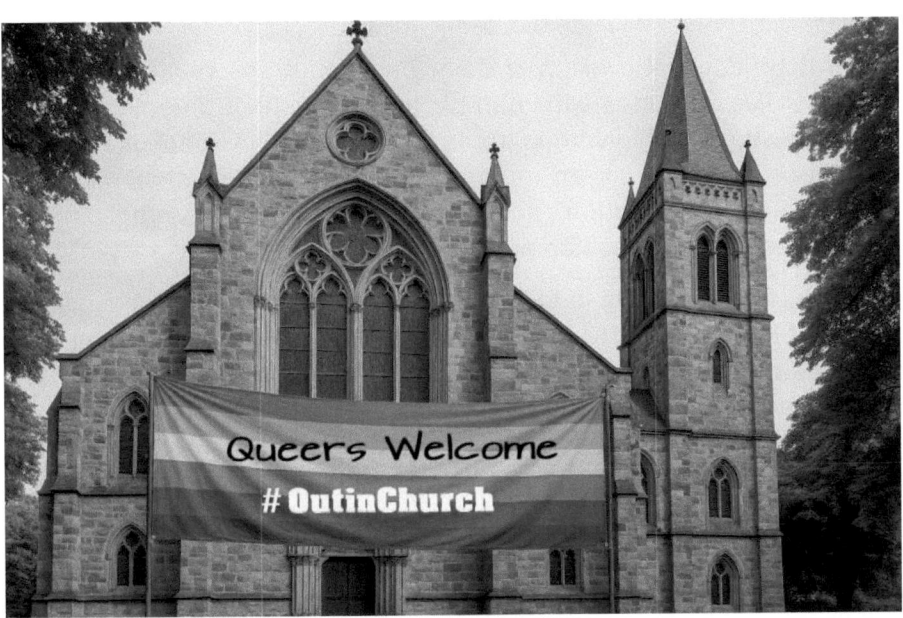

*An expressive photo of a historic church, in front of which a large rainbow flag with the inscription 'Queers Welcome #OutinChurch' is prominently displayed. The scene conveys a clear message of openness, acceptance and inclusion towards the LGBTQIA+ community. The traditional style architecture of the church provides a stark contrast to the modern message on the flag. The image is ideal for discussions about diversity, church reform, LGBTQIA+ inclusion in religious communities, and social change and tolerance.*

Of course, responsibility remains a core criterion: from the church's point of view, sexuality should be embedded in commitment, respect and fidelity - values that are ideally present in marriage. But it is becoming increasingly clear: It's not just about formal marriage boundaries, but about the quality of the relationship. Loving sexuality can be caring, respectful and life-enhancing, even if procreation is not intended. Pastors in particular report that even unmarried or unintentionally childless couples have deep spiritual experiences of unity, trust and devotion in their sexuality. These experiences challenge traditional theology to recognize God's work outside the narrow norms.

## Voices from pastoral care - experiences beyond the norm

Pastoral practice shows on a daily basis that the reality of many believers' lives collides with narrow moral teaching. People in non-marital relationships, divorced, remarried or LGBTQIA+ people - they all experience sexuality as an integral part of their lives that calls for blessing and appreciation, not taboo. For a long time, the church marginalized gay and lesbian people and labeled their love as "sin".

However, this exclusion is in blatant contradiction to the message of charity. More and more pastors and even individual bishops are therefore pushing for a new approach in dealing with queer couples. Pope Francis himself recently took steps, for example, to allow same-sex couples to be blessed under certain conditions (even if official doctrine continues to classify practiced homosexuality as sinful).

Urgent appeals are coming from pastoral care: *the church must recognize that sexuality is part of a person's identity*, emphasizes Martin Lintner.

People *"who do not correspond to the majority in sexual terms want to know that they are valued"* - anyone who loves a partner of the same sex, for example, is simply not included in previous church thinking.

This unwillingness to admit hurts and drives believers out of the church. Lintner addresses the fact that Rome often reacts defensively in its fear of opening up and misinterprets gender theories, for example, as a blanket attack on Christian anthropology.

In reality, it is about allowing everyone to *"discover their own identity and be able to stand by it"*.

Instead of coming up with rigorous prohibitions and moral codes, pastoral care should accompany individual believers *so that they can live their sexual identity responsibly and in harmony with their faith*. Or as Lintner puts it in a nutshell: *"Everyone has to find and live their own sexual identity. You can't just come up with rules that you prescribe"*.

These voices from the field - whether from moral theologians, priests or affected believers - make it clear that the church's sexual morality urgently needs to be put to the test. The gap between the official teaching and the lived reality of many believers is too great. Moral theology refers to this discrepancy as *a plausibility crisis*: the current guidelines are convincing fewer and fewer people, even well-meaning Catholics who basically share the values of the Church.

# New perspectives: feminist and queer theology of desire

In academic theology, feminist and queer approaches have developed in recent decades that positively re-evaluate desire and physicality. These contextual theologies take the experiences of women and LGBTQIA+ people seriously and read the Christian message from their perspective. This reveals something astonishing: neither the Bible nor the authentic teachings of Jesus call for the repression of sexuality - on the contrary, Jesus emphasized love, mercy and justice far more than purity rules. Queer theology shows that supposedly "homophobic" biblical passages must be understood in their historical context when analyzed closely and *not* applied to loving, consensual relationships of our time.

Rather, the Gospel invites us to integrate the marginalized and not to condemn anyone on the basis of their creation.

Feminist theologians criticize the fact that traditional sexual ethics are often permeated by patriarchal power interests - formulated by celibate men who are suspicious of female sexuality.

They reveal the extent to which the fixation on reproduction *also* served to control and domesticate female sexuality. They counter this with a positive image: Lust and female physicality as a gift from God, as a source of energy, lust for life and relational power, which is by no means sinful in itself. Thus Uta Ranke-Heinemann (as an early pioneer of this movement) calls for a sexual morality that is oriented towards people's real life circumstances instead of rigidly adhering to dogmas.

She and others see the *liberation of sexuality* from narrow rules as a step towards a church that is once again more credible, more people-friendly and more in line with Jesus.

Finally, queer theology enriches the understanding of sexuality through the perspective of diversity. It reminds us that God created humans as *diverse - "male and female he created them"* according to Genesis, but our experience also recognizes a spectrum of gender identities and orientations. Queer theologians emphasize that every loving relationship based on mutual respect and devotion can be an image of divine love - regardless of the gender or sexual orientation of the partners. In this way, previously condemned relationships can become *sacred* spaces of experience. This theology reads biblical texts "crosswise" (hence *queer*), i.e. it searches for the hidden voices of the marginalized and outsiders in the history of salvation. In doing so, it promotes an inclusive image of the church: a community in which diversity is seen as enrichment and in which physicality and love are celebrated rather than viewed with suspicion.

## Sexuality as a gift from God: a plea for integrative sexual ethics

All these developments - the reappraisal of tradition, the findings of the human sciences, the voices of those affected and the new theological approaches - lead to one conclusion: a reassessment of sexuality in the church is necessary *and* possible.

Such a re-evaluation would be more strongly oriented towards the central messages of Jesus - love, mercy, acceptance and openness.

Christian sexual ethics should be characterized less by prohibitions and more by the values proclaimed by Jesus. These include, first and foremost, love of neighbor, respect for the dignity of others and *responsibility* for one another.

There are already approaches to a more inclusive sexual ethic in other churches and in progressive Catholic circles.

These no longer start with the question of *who* is "allowed" to have sex with *whom* and under what external conditions, but ask about the quality of the relationship: Is there love, respect, fidelity, care? Are the people involved doing justice to each other? Is the sexual activity in harmony with responsibility and mutual well-being? - If so, according to a contemporary view, this lived sexuality deserves recognition as a *gift from God*, even if it takes place outside of a traditional marriage . Such an ethic would not play lust and love off against each other, but would see both as a gift to be enjoyed responsibly.

*Figure10 : Love, tenderness and sexuality even after the menopause and into old age.*

*A warm, emotional portrait of an older, happy couple laughing intimately and warmly together. The woman gently holds her partner's face as they hold their faces close together. The natural light gives the scene a golden, warm atmosphere that conveys tenderness, love and deep connection. Ideal for depicting lifelong love, happiness in old age, emotional closeness and contentment - the sexual experience of which no longer has to be tied to procreation.*

The challenges this poses for Catholic doctrine are not small. It means questioning cherished certainties and embarking on a paradigm shift - away from an often control-oriented moral teaching towards an ethic that is oriented towards people and life. But this is exactly what many committed believers and theologians are calling for. They remind us that Jesus himself was not afraid of physical closeness - he touched the sick, allowed his feet to be anointed and celebrated communal meals. Jesus never demanded sexual purity in absolute terms; what he demanded was love and truthfulness.

A church that wants to convey hope and joie de vivre must see sexuality *not* as a threat, but as a potential. Sexuality can be an expression of love, pleasure and relationship - a way for people to do good to each other and experience happiness, a place where even God's creative love can be experienced. This realization calls out to be thought through theologically. Such an integrative sexual ethic - sexuality as a gift from God that encompasses lust, love and care - could build new bridges to the church for many people. It would show that faith and joie de vivre are not opposites. And it would do justice to the claim that Jesus makes of us: to enable *life in abundance* (John 10:10).

In the end, this is a plea for an inclusive, life-oriented sexual ethic. The church would do well to stop reducing sexuality to procreation. Instead, it should learn to value the many dimensions of sexuality - as a source of strength for relationships, as an expression of love and lust, as a part of creation to which God has given his divine *"very good"*. Such a renewed view would not only take a burden off the shoulders of many believers, but would also give the church itself new credibility - as a place that proclaims love without conditions and affirms the whole of humanity.

Because beyond shame, guilt and exclusion, a church can grow that is hopeful, accepting and reconciling - and *hope* lives in community: with love, without reservations.

# Chapter 7:
# Does the Taboo on Sexuality Promote Sexual Abuse in the Catholic Priesthood?

*The chapter addresses the effects of the taboo on sexuality within the Catholic Church on sexual abuse by clergy. Historically, the traditional anti-sexual attitude, coupled with mandatory celibacy, led to a climate of silence, shame and repressed sexuality. Experts emphasize that the central problem is not celibacy itself, but the deeply rooted and repressed sexual morality. The lack of open discussion of sexuality in priestly training and church life has created a culture in which abuse often remains hidden. International abuse scandals, such as in the USA, Ireland, Chile, Germany and Australia, showed patterns of cover-up, transfer of accused priests and systematic secrecy. For a long time, these mechanisms prevented the effective prevention and investigation of abuse. A fundamental change is required: away from tabooing and towards a transparent, responsible and sex education-based culture.*

- *Question: What specific cultural and structural changes are necessary for the Catholic Church to prevent sexual abuse in the future and at the same time promote an open, responsible approach to sexuality?*
- *Question: Isn't the ongoing taboo on sexuality within the Catholic Church ultimately a protective mechanism to safeguard hierarchical power structures - even at the expense of victims of sexual abuse?*
- *Option for action: The Catholic Church should immediately establish comprehensive sex education programs in all church educational institutions and seminaries, accompanied by transparent reporting procedures and independent monitoring mechanisms to prevent sexual abuse and effectively protect victims, and abolish celibacy.*

- **Training option:** *Clergy, believers and pupils in religious education should acquire skills in sexual education, trauma sensitivity and dealing with power and responsibility through targeted training courses and workshops. In addition, they should be trained to speak openly about sexuality, celibacy and abuse, to break down taboos and actively support effective prevention.*

For centuries, sexuality was considered a sensitive, even sinful topic in the Catholic Church - especially for priests. Mandatory celibacy and a moral doctrine hostile to sexuality created a climate of silence and shame. Could this tabooing of sexuality have encouraged the sexual abuse of children and young people by Catholic clergy? The following article sheds light on the connection between church sexual morals, power structures and abuse, provides an overview of major abuse scandals worldwide and asks for necessary cultural and structural changes. A theological reflection on power, guilt, sin, protection and responsibility should help to understand what needs to change so that the church can live up to its claim to be a place of protection.

## Anti-sex culture, celibacy and taboo - a dangerous mix?

For a long time, Catholic moral teaching viewed sexuality primarily in the context of sin and procreation. Lust and physical love were often viewed with suspicion. Abstinence is required of clerics in particular - celibacy is compulsory for priests of the Latin Church. However, critics point out that this strict sexual morality has problematic side effects. Church historians, for example, have attributed the celibacy requirement with promoting sexual abuse since the Middle Ages.

On the other hand, experts emphasize that the deeper problem is a repressed sexual morality overall - celibacy is *"only a symptom, not the cause"*.

In other words, a culture that represses and taboos sexuality creates an unnatural environment in which sexual needs can shift into the shadows and break out in unhealthy ways.

In fact, a problematic attitude is still evident in the training of Catholic priests today: sexual topics are excluded. In 2024, an independent commission in the Archdiocese of Freiburg found that sexuality was "still a taboo" in the training of priests.

Important aspects such as dealing with celibacy or the question of homosexuality are not dealt with sufficiently. Seminarians feel left alone with their questions and conflicts. According to the experts, this lack of openness not only makes it more difficult to identify problematic tendencies (such as pedosexual tendencies) in prospective priests, but also to support victims of abuse.

In short: where sexuality is taboo, healthy learning processes and corrective measures are lacking. Priests run the risk of developing an immature or repressed sexuality - a risk factor that can have fatal consequences when combined with power imbalances.

# Silence, shame and clerical power structures as a breeding ground

Closely linked to sexual hostility is a culture of silence and shame. For a long time, sexuality and abuse were not talked about openly in the church - out of a sense of shame and fear of scandal. This silence runs through many levels: From believers not daring to address intimate problems to victims not daring to report assaults. Clerical power structures also play a role. Priests and bishops traditionally enjoyed great authority; their words were not contradicted. In such authoritarian structures, it is particularly difficult for those affected to make themselves heard. The hierarchy tends to fear its own loss of authority - and sweep some things under the carpet.

Lisa Kötter, co-founder of the church-reflective initiative Maria 2.0, describes it like this: when it comes to abuse, the Catholic Church behaves in an "authoritarian manner" and does not feel accountable - "hence the silence". Silence is used as a *"powerful weapon"* in the hope that the matter will grow over time. In the end, this culture of silence does not protect the victims, but the perpetrators and the institution.

From a theological perspective, this creates a vicious circle: a lack of information and open taboos lead to those affected remaining alone with their conflicts or seeking guidance in questionable ways. The following sentence sums it up: *A lack of information or taboos can also lead to people seeking advice from questionable sources or repressed conflicts arising. In extreme cases, strict taboos can also encourage abuse by creating a culture of silence in which those affected do not dare to speak about the injustice they have experienced.*

Such a culture of looking the other way and keeping quiet favors perpetrators: they can act almost unchallenged, while victims are silenced by shame. When authority becomes more important than truth and control is placed above compassion, as the church has done for a long time, this paves the way for hidden abuse.

## Global abuse scandals and how to deal with them

The Catholic Church has been rocked by serious abuse scandals in numerous countries, which often only came to light decades later. Since the 2000s, systematic cases of sexualized violence have been uncovered in countries such as the USA, Ireland, Chile, Germany and Australia. These revelations caused worldwide horror, led to public apologies from church leaders and the first steps towards coming to terms with the past. Below is an overview of five of the best-known cases and the status of the investigation:

- **USA (Boston)** - In 2002, journalists from the *Boston Globe* uncovered that priests in the Archdiocese of Boston had been abusing underage victims for decades and had been covered up by their superiors. Documents proved that the diocese leadership simply transferred the perpetrators instead of intervening, despite being aware of the allegations.

The scandal spread to the entire USA: Thousands of cases became known, several dioceses filed for bankruptcy in order to make compensation payments (totaling over 3 billion dollars) to the victims. The archbishop responsible for Boston, Cardinal Bernard Law, resigned as a result of the revelations.

In 2002, the US Conference of Catholic Bishops adopted the "Dallas Charter" with strict guidelines for the protection of children. Nevertheless, subsequent investigations - such as a 2018 grand jury report in Pennsylvania with over 300 accused priests - show that the process of coming to terms with this remains a lengthy one.

- **Ireland** - In Ireland, state commissions of inquiry revealed a staggering extent of abuse in church institutions. The Ryan Report (2009) documented decades of *"endemic"* abuse in children's homes, orphanages and schools run by Catholic orders.

Thousands of boys and girls were raped, beaten and humiliated. At the same time, it emerged that the Irish church leadership had protected pedocriminals from prosecution.

The Murphy Report, also published in 2009, revealed cases of cover-ups in the Archdiocese of Dublin. These revelations led to a drastic loss of trust in the Irish church: bishops resigned, the Pope apologized to the victims in a pastoral letter in 2010 and the state set up compensation funds.

Ireland thus became a pioneer in coming to terms with the past, inspiring many other countries - but this can only partially alleviate the suffering of the victims.

- **Chile** - In Chile, the church became the center of an abuse scandal in 2010 with the case of Fernando Karadima. Karadima, a charismatic priest and influential mentor to several bishops, had sexually abused boys for decades - under the watchful eyes of church superiors who protected him.

Only the persistent testimony of victims brought the case to light, but initially even Pope Francis held a protective hand over an accused bishop. In 2018, a historic step was finally taken: all 34 Chilean bishops offered their resignations following talks with the Pope. Francis accepted several resignations and instructed the remaining bishops to carry out comprehensive reforms. Karadima himself was dismissed from the clergy.

The Chilean scandal made it clear that abuse is not a "local" problem, but has structural causes - and that only radical transparency and personal consequences can win back the trust of the faithful.

- **Germany** - A wave of abuse cases also emerged in Germany in 2010, triggered by the discovery of decades of abuse at the Jesuit school Canisius-Kolleg in Berlin.

In the following months, hundreds of victims from almost all dioceses came forward. The German Bishops' Conference then commissioned a scientific study. This so-called MHG study (2018) produced alarming figures: Between 1946 and 2014, there were at least 3,677 underage victims of sexual abuse and 1,670 accused clerics in German dioceses.

According to the study, around 4.4% of all priests during this period abused minors. The study also identified facilitating factors, including "asymmetrical power relations" and a closed institutional system.

In the meantime, individual dioceses - such as Cologne, Munich and Münster - have presented their own expert reports, which also heavily incriminate prominent churchmen. The process of coming to terms with the past is underway, but remains difficult: many victims complain that compensation has been slow and there have been too few structural changes. Nevertheless, the immense public pressure has led to initiatives such as the "Synodal Path", in which clergy and laity discuss reform proposals (from sexual morality to the distribution of power).

- **Australia** - The Australian Royal Commission (Commission of Inquiry) painted a particularly shocking picture in its final report in 2017. It found that 7% of all Catholic priests in Australia were accused of child sexual abuse between 1950 and 2010

A total of 4,444 victims reported assaults in a church context - in parishes, boarding schools, orphanages and schools, some of which were committed by up to 15% of priests in individual dioceses. The average victims were boys aged 11.

These figures shocked the country. The commission found that church leaders had often placed the protection of the institution above the welfare of the child. The Australian church apologized and introduced reforms, such as stricter checks and training. At the same time, cases were prosecuted - prominently, for example, that of Cardinal George Pell, formerly Australia's highest Catholic dignitary (his conviction for abuse was overturned by the High Court in 2020 due to lack of evidence). The Australian report is one of the most comprehensive investigations worldwide and is forcing the church to radically question its structures.

These five cases exemplify a worldwide problem. A similar pattern can be seen everywhere: clerics abuse their power and sexuality in secret, the institution initially reacts defensively or cover-up until public pressure leads to action. But what exactly did these cover-up mechanisms look like? And what needs to change to prevent such acts in the future?

Mothers may come to the realization that they should no longer entrust their young children and adolescents to the local clergy in the parish.

## Cover-up: When the reputation was more important than the victims

The sad truth is that in many cases the church not only failed to protect the most vulnerable, but actively contributed to the cover-up of crimes. Several strategies were typical:

**Transfer of offenders:** Instead of pressing charges or removing an accused priest from circulation, he was often simply transferred quietly to another parish or even abroad. This "rotation" principle was intended to avoid scandals, but perpetuated the crimes elsewhere. In 2014, a UN report accused the Vatican of covering up crimes through precisely this practice.

Priests were subject to a "code of silence" to prevent them from turning to the police. In this way, perpetrators were protected while communities were kept in the dark.

**Secret archives and file destruction:** Allegations of abuse often ended up in secret church files that remained hidden from the public and state justice (partly supported by Vatican regulations such as the now relaxed *"Papal Secret"* for internal church abuse proceedings). In Germany, the MHG study found evidence that files were manipulated or deleted in order to erase traces of abuse.

In many cases, incidents were not even recorded, but "settled" internally. This lack of transparency made it almost impossible for victims to obtain justice and enabled accused clerics to continue working without reproach.

**Pressure on victims:** Numerous victims report how they were pressured into silence. In some cases, parents were advised not to make the matter public "in the interests of the church". Or compensation was only paid on the condition of strict confidentiality. The church's reflex to protect its own reputation led to cold-hearted reactions towards the victims. The dignity of those affected was betrayed in order to preserve the image of the institution.

This moral failure still weighs heavily on the church today - it is as if it has turned the gospel of compassion and justice on its head. A perverted church.

The mechanisms mentioned - silence, denial, transfer, shredding files - show a systemic failure. The institution prioritized its own existence over the suffering of children and young people. This is precisely what Pope Francis criticized in 2018 in a much-noticed letter *"to the people of God"*, in which he denounced a "culture of death" through cover-ups and called on all believers to adopt zero tolerance. A long road of reappraisal is needed to overcome this misconduct. But what specific changes are needed to prevent abuse in the best possible way in the future?

## Prevention: cultural and structural change is key

Several demands for the future can be derived from the findings of the scandals. Prevention of abuse must take a holistic approach - culturally, educationally and structurally. Important starting points are:

- **Sexuality education and de-tabooed sex education:** Sexuality should no longer be a taboo subject in the church. Neither in priest training nor in catechetical teaching should sexuality be discussed in a coy or moralistic manner. Instead, there is a need for sound sexual education that helps future priests to integrate their own sexuality in a mature and responsible way. Consequently, celibacy should be abolished - also as a sign of change. Talking openly about feelings, boundaries, lust and chastity must be a natural part of training.

Only in this way can problematic tendencies be recognized or dealt with at an early stage. The same applies to general church education work: young people in schools and parishes should receive age-appropriate sexual ethics education that does not create fear, but provides guidance. An open culture of discussion - in the confession room, classroom and family - also enables those affected to name assaults more quickly, without shame or taboo.

- **Transparency and accountability:** The days of secrecy must end. In the event of allegations of sexualized violence, the state justice system must be called in immediately - there must be no more silence within the church. Institutionally, there is a need for independent investigative commissions (as have been set up in many countries) that have access to all files. The church must actively publish information about incidents and make transparent what consequences have been drawn. Bishops and religious superiors, in turn, must be held accountable for their actions or inactions. This principle of accountability has long been alien to the hierarchical church - it requires a rethink in the leadership culture.

- **Training for those in positions of responsibility:** Prevention is a top priority. From pastors to bishops, all church leaders should undergo mandatory training on child protection and dealing with cases of abuse. Many dioceses have already made improvements here, but continuous training in psychology, trauma pedagogy and law is needed. Those who train future priests must also be trained accordingly in order to counteract taboo tendencies. Recognizing perpetrators is a particular challenge: Expertise and attentiveness are required here so that warning signs are not overlooked. Training can help to recognize manipulative behaviour or grooming strategies, for example.

- **Limitation of power and control:** Structurally, the church must distribute power and make the abuse of power more difficult. This includes stronger participation rights for laypeople in parishes and church committees so that male clerics are not able to exercise uncontrolled control. External supervision (e.g. by state authorities or independent representatives) can also be useful in order to form a counterweight to the hierarchy within the church. Many reform movements - such as the Synodal Way in Germany or international initiatives such as *We Are Church* - are calling for the unbundling of ministries and more checks and balances. The message is clear: a monocratic, *"monarchical"* structure without transparency, as Lisa Kötter deplores, invites abuse. This can be counteracted by steps towards democratization.

- **Greater and equal participation of women:** One of the loudest calls is for women to be much more equally involved in leadership roles and decision-making processes in the church. The exaggeration of the male ordained ministry and the exclusion of women from positions of power have created a clerical male world in which toxic dynamics could develop. More women in roles of responsibility - as prevention officers, in administrative leadership positions, as deacons or priests (according to the demands of the expert reform groups) - could change the culture permanently. Women bring in other perspectives and are more likely to break down the *"wall of silence"*. Abbot Peter von Sury (Mariastein Monastery) emphasizes: *"It is essential that we men learn to listen to women."*

This learning process has begun: Pope Francis has appointed women to high curia offices for the first time, and many dioceses around the world are empowering women in key roles. In the long term, a more balanced gender distribution in church leadership should help to prevent abuse - if only because power would no longer be so one-sidedly concentrated.

- **Correction of sexual morality:** Finally, the church's sexual ethics themselves are also up for debate. As long as certain realities of life (such as homosexuality, remarried divorcees, contraception) are branded as sin across the board, a climate of guilt and repression is created among many believers. In the past, the church's sexual morality often led to feelings of guilt, repression and double standards, according to many analyses.

A contemporary, positive sexual ethic that focuses on love, responsibility and consensus instead of prohibitions would create a *climate of acceptance instead of guilt.*

This would also take pressure off the clergy, who would no longer have to regard human sexuality as an "enemy". The Synodal Path in Germany has already drawn up reform texts in this area that call for a re-evaluation of homosexuality and a rejection of repressive moralism and celibacy. A cultural change in sexual morality could ultimately also prevent abuse, as less repression and double lives would be necessary.

Figure11 : Priest and a child who cannot yet break the silence.

*A condensed, minimalist illustration that addresses the serious topic of abuse and silence in the church. In the foreground is a sad boy with his eyes closed and tape over his mouth, symbolizing silence. Behind him is a priest with a lowered gaze, whose posture suggests power and control. On the left-hand side, we see praying hands pointing towards a cross, which emphasizes the religious dimension. The illustration uses dark, muted colors, especially shades of purple and black, to create an oppressive and critical atmosphere. The image is suitable for discussions about institutional sexual abuse, responsibility and silence in religious contexts - as well as for discussing the timely abolition of celibacy.*

All of these preventative approaches boil down to one thing: the church must step down from its high claim to power and place humble service to people in the foreground. Only in a church that looks honestly, listens and shares responsibility will sexual offenders no longer have an easy time of it.

## Theological reflection: power, guilt, sin - and responsibility

The abuse crisis is not only an institutional failure, but also a spiritual and theological challenge. How could a church that proclaims the gospel of love and care become so guilty? A relentless reappraisal must shed light on the categories of power, guilt, sin, protection and responsibility.

**Power and powerlessness:** Jesus told his disciples that whoever wants to be first should be the servant of all. This principle was perverted during the abuse crisis: Clergymen shamelessly abused their power over those under their protection. This demonstrates *hubris* - priests placed themselves above those entrusted to their care, sometimes with the feeling that they were acting in the name of God, as Abbot von Sury notes.

This clerical power imbalance, supported by hierarchy and clericalism, proved to be disastrous. Theologically speaking, power in the church is only legitimate if it is exercised as a service. Where power becomes domination and an end in itself, it degenerates and turns into an abuse of power. The church must ask itself how its structures of power are compatible with the example of Christ - and where they are not, it must dare to reform. Feminist and liberation theology approaches in particular have long criticized patriarchal power structures as incompatible with the Gospel. The abuse scandals tragically prove them right.

**Guilt and sin:** Sexual abuse of children and those under our protection is undoubtedly a grave sin. But it is not just about the individual guilt of the perpetrators. The institution of the church is also guilty - by looking away, covering up and being cold towards the victims.

*The Church has made itself guilty by not acting as a guardian of life, but by contributing to guilt and suffering. Its true vocation - protection, justice, truth and mercy - has been turned upside down in such contexts.* This formulation sums it up theologically: the church has betrayed its calling when, instead of offering protection and truth, it itself causes guilt and suffering. The church's sin here consists of omission and cover-up - a structural context of sin that made many individual acts possible in the first place. Asking for forgiveness is not enough; this guilt must be acknowledged and cleared up. This includes repenting, doing justice to the victims and drawing consequences. Where this is refused, the guilt remains. In his letter to Ireland in 2010, Pope Benedict XVI stated that the Church must also confess and repent of the *"sins of its pastors"*. This shows that classic concepts such as sin and repentance are highly topical: The Church needs a deep conversion (*metanoia*) in order to move from the sin of cover-up to the virtue of truth.

**Protective mission:** In the Bible, Jesus places a child in the center and says: *"Whoever welcomes one of these little ones in my name welcomes me."* Protecting the welfare of children is therefore the core mission of the church. This makes it all the more appalling that children were harmed in the church of all places. Theologically, one could say that the church has failed if it does not protect the defenceless. *If strict taboos create a climate in which those affected are afraid to speak out, perpetrators are protected and systematic looking away is encouraged, then the institution is overstepping its responsibility towards those in need of protection and the Gospel itself* - or so the warning goes.

This is exactly what has happened: Through silence and tabooing, the church has denied its charges the protection they need. Instead of being a *safe haven*, in some places it has become a danger zone. Theologically, the church's mandate to protect can be derived from its self-image: As the *"people of God"* and the *"body of Christ"*, it must ensure that every member of this body is protected from harm. A member that suffers (the abused child) affects the whole body. In future, this protection mandate must have absolute priority - over the protection of one's own reputation or even over the protection of the perpetrator. There must be no more ambiguity here.

**Responsibility and repentance:** Responsibility arises from guilt. It is not enough to condemn individual *"black sheep"*, the institution itself must take responsibility. *True responsibility begins where this guilt is not relativized, but named, acknowledged and addressed in concrete terms - not just through words, but through transparent reforms, genuine reappraisal and listening to those affected.*

This insight demands action: real reappraisal, structural reforms and, above all, closeness to the victims. Acting responsibly means listening to the victims, enduring their stories and drawing consequences - even if it costs the church something. Responsibility also means facing up to the state authorities and allowing justice beyond one's control. In biblical language, it is about repentance: The church must change from an *institution of fear and secrecy* to a *community of openness and care*. This is a painful process, but one that enables healing. Some religious communities have given space to rituals of repentance and healing - such as public confessions of guilt in the presence of victims. Such steps have a deep symbolic and spiritual meaning: they show that one calls sin by its name and repents before God and man. Only from this can new trust grow.

From a theological perspective, the abuse crisis calls on the church to become humble again. It must recognize that ministers are also sinners and need to be controlled. It must share power, confess guilt, ask for forgiveness and do everything possible to prevent future sins of this kind. Basically, it is about nothing less than a *renewal from within*, a cultural and spiritual change. Those pleas for forgiveness that popes and bishops have formulated must not remain cheap - they must be filled with life through reforms and a new ethic of mindfulness.

**Action option:** Finally, a concrete measure that can be proposed is to establish a comprehensive, sex education-based and transparency-oriented culture of coming to terms with sexualized violence in all church educational institutions - from schools and boarding schools to seminaries for priests. Each of these institutions should establish programs for the prevention and processing of sexualized violence that are pedagogically accompanied and spiritually flanked. This means, for example, ongoing training for employees in child protection, age-appropriate education for children and young people, easily accessible reporting systems for suspected cases, external contact persons for those affected and regular reflection on the topic in the light of the Gospel. Spiritual support for these processes ensures that the process is not only legal and administrative, but also pastoral - with prayer, rituals of healing and forgiveness where appropriate. Such measures can help to break through the culture of secrecy and create a space in which healing can take place. The church would send a signal that it has learned from its mistakes: it takes the perspective of the victims, honestly deals with the past and shapes the future in such a way that abuse no longer has a place. Parents may come to the realization that they can no longer leave their children and young people unattended and unsupervised in the hands and community of the clergy. The future goal is therefore a church that is a safe place for everyone - *"Church* *must be a safe place for everyone. This is what we are working towards",* as the Vicar General of Freiburg aptly put it.

All reforms, all theology and all pastoral action must be subordinated to this goal. The crisis can thus become a turning point: Away from taboo and abuse as well as celibacy, towards openness, responsibility and protection - so that such a failure is never repeated.

The unanimous and central finding remains: the tabooing of sexuality and authoritarian structures have facilitated abuse in the Catholic Church - but through honest reappraisal and reforms, the Church can learn from this and live up to its responsibility.

# Chapter 8:
# Is Catholic sexual morality beneficial to life - or distant from it?

*The chapter examines traditional Catholic sexual morality in terms of its usefulness for life. Historically, this morality is based on a historical approach that reduces sexuality primarily to procreation and rejects all sexual acts outside of a sacramental marriage as well as the use of artificial contraceptives. This position of the Church, manifested above all in the encyclical "Humanae Vitae" by Pope Paul VI in 1968, is increasingly perceived in today's society as distant from life and out of date. Critical voices argue that such morals hinder healthy sexual development, promote feelings of guilt and ignore the reality of many believers. Modern human scientific and theological findings emphasize sexuality as an expression of love, relationship and joie de vivre, which goes far beyond purely reproductive purposes and therefore also has spiritual and emotional dimensions. A cultural shift towards an integrative and life-oriented sexual ethic that takes greater account of personal conscience and the diversity of human relationships is increasingly being called for.*

- *Question: To what extent is it possible for the Catholic Church to further develop its sexual morality in such a way that it seriously recognizes the diverse realities and needs of people's lives and at the same time does justice to its spiritual mission?*
- *Question: Is a sexual morality that primarily evaluates love and sexuality as a potential danger and moral trap not rather life-denying than life-serving, and thus ultimately betrays the central Christian message of the fullness of life?*
- *Option for action: The Catholic Church should undertake a fundamental reassessment of its sexual ethics, by detaching sexuality from its exclusive connection to procreation and instead establishing an ethic of responsibility, love and*

emotional integrity that is oriented towards real contexts of love and life.

- **Training option:** Clergy, believers and students in religious education should acquire skills in holistic sexual education, ethical reflection and responsible relationship management through specific educational programs. Seminars and workshops on psychosexual development, gender-sensitive theology and communication training should be offered in order to be able to authentically and credibly accompany the transition to a contemporary and humane sexual ethic.

Catholic sexual morality is due for further development or revision following the crossfire of criticism: Many believers feel that the official regulations are unrealistic and hardly useful for life. What the church teaches often clashes with what people today consider to be a responsible love life. For example, intimate cohabitation before marriage has long been considered normal for most Catholic couples - it is estimated that around 90 percent live together and share sexuality before the wedding ceremony.

At the same time, young believers in particular feel pressured by rigid guidelines or burdened with feelings of guilt. Against this backdrop, the question is growing: do the church's sexual ethics really serve life and love - or are they distancing themselves from the reality of people's lives?

The tensions are not only evident in the everyday lives of believers, but also in the institutional church. While official teaching leaves little room for maneuver, there are increasing voices from theology and the grassroots calling for a reorientation of sexual morality. In the following, the foundations of Catholic sexual doctrine are presented, criticism from a reform-oriented perspective is examined and theological arguments for a renewed sexual ethic are presented. We also look at the demands of the Synodal Path in Germany and incorporate queer, feminist and relational ethical perspectives. The result is a draft of sexual ethics that places responsibility, love and self-determination above blind obedience - as an expression of mature faith practice in the 21st century.

## Official sexual morality: what the Catechism teaches

The Church's teaching on sexuality is clearly formulated in the *Catechism of the Catholic Church* and in magisterial documents. It follows a traditional basic principle: sexual acts are only permitted within marriage between a man and a woman and should be open to the possibility of the procreation of new life. The Catechism literally states: *"The sexual act may only take place within marriage; outside of marriage it is always a grave sin."*

Sexuality is thus closely linked to marriage and procreation; the Church classifies anything that deviates from this as sinful. Accordingly, the Church not only condemns homosexual acts as disorderly, but also extramarital sex, masturbation and artificial contraception as incompatible with the divine order.

This sexual morality is based on historical thinking: what is considered the "natural" purpose of sexuality - namely love between a man and a woman in marriage and procreation - is set as morally absolute. Traditional teaching rejects anything "unnatural" (such as contraception or same-sex acts).

At the same time, the church emphasizes values such as chastity and abstinence: sexual abstinence before marriage and sexual fidelity in marriage are considered the ideal. Lust and passion have their place within this framework, but only if they are embedded in conjugal love and directed towards procreation. This official line has been defended by the Church's magisterium for decades - most recently in the encyclical *Humanae Vitae* (1968) or in the Catechism (first edition 1992) - and it remains formally unchanged to this day.

## Between ideal and reality: criticism of rigid sexual ethics

In fact, many believers experience this strict sexual morality as distant from life rather than beneficial to it. There is an enormous gap between the ideal held up and the reality lived out. Priests who marry young couples openly report that hardly anyone remains abstinent without getting married - even practicing Catholics usually only see *abstinence before marriage* as a theoretical ideal, not a realistic expectation.

The result is a widespread *ignoring* of doctrine: believers decide independently about contraception or their cohabitation, often without even seriously considering the church's verdict. As a result, sexual morality is effectively losing its binding force in the everyday lives of many - and the gap between the Magisterium and the faithful is growing.

But this does not stop at tacit disregard. Reform-oriented theologians are clearly critical of traditional sexual ethics. Above all, they criticize its rigid logic of prohibition and focus on sin and guilt. For centuries, the church has branded a large part of human sexuality as sinful across the board - which has led to a fearful morality among many believers. Young people in particular, or those who do not conform to the heterosexual ideal, felt and still feel marginalized as a result. The fixation on rules ("Thou shalt not...") places prohibitions above individual decisions of conscience and therefore does not do justice to the complexity of human relationships.

Many critics also see traditional sexual morality as a power factor: according to the accusation, it has long served to control physicality and women's sexuality in particular. The dogmatist Julia Knop - herself a member of the German Synodal Path - describes it as *"truly catastrophic"* that some bishops continue to *"show no willingness to let go of their desire to control bodies, control women, control sexuality."*

Such morality, which primarily insists on obedience to rules instead of accompanying people in their responsible loving relationship, appears outdated from a reform-oriented perspective. Even more: in the preparation of the Synodal Path, it was openly stated that the previous sexual ethics even had a negative influence - it had created a climate in which double standards and taboos could flourish and thus encouraged abuse in the church.

If sexuality is only repressed and forbidden, destructive forms seek their way in secret.

Critics are therefore calling for an end to the guilt-ridden morality of prohibition. It should be replaced by a philanthropic sexual ethic that takes the reality of believers seriously and encourages them to deal with sexuality responsibly without moralistic undertones. Away from fear and towards a culture in which sexuality is neither glorified nor demonized, but rather integrated into the practice of faith as an integral part of life.

## Love, responsibility and conscience: A plea for a new sexual ethics

In view of the shortcomings of the old sexual morality, many theologians are calling for a paradigm shift towards a sexual ethic that focuses on love, responsibility and personal conscience. Because from a Christian perspective, love is the highest commandment - every ethic of sexuality must be measured against whether it promotes or hinders love. Sexuality should serve life by being an expression of love and connection. Although Pope John Paul II emphasized the dignity of marital sexuality in his *Theology of the Body,* he insisted on the traditional boundaries. Today, progressive theologians go one step further: they ask whether rules that prevent loving relationships or unnecessarily burden people really correspond to the Gospel.

One prominent representative of this reform perspective was the moral theologian Eberhard Schockenhoff. He urged the Catholic magisterium to rethink and spoke of a necessary paradigm shift. Schockenhoff opposed a narrowing of moral teaching to mere prohibitions and made it clear that church doctrines on sexuality were *not* immutable natural laws of God. If certain statements of sexual morality did not help to lead people to God or make it possible for them to experience God's love, then *"the annoying obstacle to faith* must be *removed by revising the church's teaching on this point."*

In other words, rules that no longer serve any recognizable commandment of love must not be an end in themselves.

Schockenhoff and other theologians outline the basic lines of a new sexual ethic in such a way that sexuality is appreciated in all its dimensions. It should no longer be reduced to its *"primary natural purpose"* of procreation - instead, the church must recognize the *"diversity of meaningful dimensions of sexuality".*

This includes the importance of sexuality for the couple relationship - for example as an expression of love, intimacy and trust - and its contribution to the development of a person's identity. Sexuality has emotional, physical mental and social aspects that go beyond the biological aspect of procreation. A sexual morality that wants to be beneficial to life must integrate all of these aspects.

In concrete terms, this means that the focus is on the *quality of the relationship* and the values practiced within it - respect, commitment, fidelity, equality and care. Whether a couple is married or not, whether they are heterosexual or homosexual, takes a back seat as a moral criterion. From an ethical point of view, the decisive factor is how people live their sexuality: whether in love and mutual respect or at the expense of the other. This attitude corresponds to a relationship ethic that is increasingly replacing the classic morality of prohibition. For example, a survey of theology students showed that a large majority reject traditional statements such as "sexual devotion is *only* possible in marriage in all its truth"; instead, students find anything *"that corresponds to the right to personal, free, sexual self-determination"* plausible.

The signal is clear: self-determined love in responsibility should be the guiding principle, not primarily obedience to old norms.

# Pressure for reform in the church: The synodal path and new approaches

These demands for a new sexual ethic are far from merely theoretical. In the Catholic Church in Germany, a broad reform process has taken shape with the Synodal Path (2019-2023), which has also put the church's sexual morals to the test. Triggered by the investigation into the abuse scandal, the church dared *to take a self-critical stance* on its teachings on love, sexuality and partnership.

In some cases, far-reaching reform proposals were put forward that would have seemed unthinkable just a few years ago.

A central text of the Synodal Path - the basic text *"Living in Successful Relationships - Basic Lines of a Renewed Sexual Ethic"* - formulated new emphases on sexual doctrine. Among other things, sexuality was to be re-evaluated *beyond* the narrow norm of marriage. For example, proposed that sex outside of marriage and masturbation should no longer be classified as a sin across the board.

Non-heterosexual love relationships should also be recognized by the church as valuable and equal. For the first time, there was even talk of the church recognizing the existence of *different gender identities* beyond the binary order.

In the preamble to this reform paper, it was unequivocally stated: *"Church sexual ethics [with its previous orientation] has facilitated the crimes of sexualized violence in the church."*

A sharp diagnosis that makes it clear why change is urgently needed.

The Synodal Assembly called for two things in this context: firstly, for the German bishops to take steps in their area of responsibility - for example, to enable blessings for couples *beyond sacramental marriage* (for example, for remarried divorcees or same-sex couples). In fact, some dioceses have already begun to make such blessings a pastoral reality. Secondly, the assembly recommended that the Pope reassess certain doctrinal issues of sexual morality worldwide.

This explicitly included a revision of the stance on contraception and a re-evaluation of the sacrament of marriage for same-sex lovers.

In plain language: the relevant passages of the Catechism - such as the statement that homosexual acts are "in no case to be condoned" - may no longer stand up to today's theological and human scientific knowledge and should be changed.

However, the debates were not without resistance. A scandal occurred when the basic text on sexual morality was defeated by a blocking minority of conservative bishops at the synodal assembly in September 2022.

Around 40% of the bishops refused to approve the reform paper - enough to fall short of the required two-thirds vote of the bishops in accordance with the statutes. The shock among the reform-oriented synod members was great: many were stunned that so many older bishops remained immovable when it came to sexual morality of all things.

Thomas Söding, professor of theology and Vice President of the Synodal Path, spoke of an *"intellectual disaster"*.

He suspected that the statements on gender diversity and active sexuality outside of marriage had simply gone too far for some bishops.

This shows that Catholic ethics, with its fixed model of gender and norms, has enormous difficulties in integrating the findings of biology and the human sciences on intersexuality, trans identity and modern partnership culture.

Despite this setback - combined with the need to wait for further years of demographic change - the Synodal Way was ultimately able to pass a number of resolutions urging change. For example, a majority of the congregation later voted in favor of introducing blessings for loving couples regardless of their marriage certificate and for a revision of the church's employment law so that no one loses their church ministry position due to their private lifestyle (e.g. a same-sex partnership). This will also have an impact on celibacy, as it also affects the private love and lifestyle of clergy.

And even if not all reform proposals can be implemented immediately - many lie within the decision-making authority of the Vatican with its many old white men - this process has nevertheless achieved something fundamental: The Church in Germany has sought to connect with the real world and initiated debates that are being held worldwide. More and more believers and pastors are signaling that the traditional sexual morality in its current form is no longer sustainable. What is needed is a sexual ethic that accepts and respects the reality of people's lives - as formulated by numerous Catholic associations in January 2022 in support of the initiative #OutInChurch. This broad call for renewal shows that the topic has reached the heart of the church.

## Integrating queer and feminist perspectives

Queer and feminist perspectives play a crucial role in the debate about contemporary sexual morality. In recent years, queer people - i.e. LGBTQIA+ people - have impressively demonstrated to the church the consequences of marginalizing sexual norms. The *#OutInChurch* initiative, for example, in which a total of 125 employees of the Catholic Church publicly acknowledged their non-heterosexual identity at the beginning of 2022, denounced the discrimination and fear suffered by many of those affected. Their demand: a church *"in which all Christians are welcome"* and which sees diversity as an enrichment.

This includes no longer defaming same-sex love as a sin. From a queer theological perspective, love before God is not bound to a specific gender pattern. Two people of the same sex can have just as deep, responsible and beneficial a love relationship as heterosexual couples. A sexual morality that wants to be beneficial to life should therefore recognize and support such relationships instead of condemning them. Changes can already be seen in practice: Some courageous pastors have blessed same-sex couples (despite the Vatican's "no" to such blessings near the sacrament of marriage), and acceptance is growing in parishes. Queer Catholics emphasize that they know they are loved by God but often do not feel accepted by the Church - this pain calls for reconciliation and doctrinal change.

Feminist theologians also criticize traditional sexual morality. They make it clear that this teaching was historically strongly influenced by a male-clerical view that wanted to control female sexuality. The strict rejection of artificial contraception, for example, affected and still affects women in a particular way, as they carry pregnancies to term. The ban on the pill (enshrined in *Humanae Vitae*) was met with worldwide resistance - to this day, it is ignored by the majority of Catholic couples. Feminist criticism sees a patriarchal pattern behind such bans: sexuality was viewed primarily in terms of *reproduction*, which reduces the role of women to motherhood and restricts their sexual autonomy. For a long time, women's lust and desire received little positive attention in church teachings. In addition, women were often addressed as guardians of chastity - the responsibility for sexual "purity" was often culturally placed on their shoulders. Contemporary sexual ethics must therefore take gender justice into account. It must take women and men (and people beyond this binary thinking) equally seriously in their own sexual needs and boundaries. Every person has the right to dispose of their own body and the duty to respect the dignity of others - these are principles that should be anchored in a renewed doctrine.

Queer and feminist approaches equally emphasize the importance of a relationship ethic that does not focus on fulfilling traditional roles or norms, but on the quality of the relationship and the well-being of those involved. They ask: Does a certain kind of sexuality create *life in abundance* for the partners? Does it promote equality, is it based on consensus and mutual love? This is the measure of whether it is morally responsible - not dogmatic criteria such as a marriage certificate or the intention to procreate alone. By integrating these perspectives, sexual morality can become more inclusive, just and compassionate. After all, the argument goes, Jesus himself accepted the marginalized and broke rigid purity laws - in this spirit, it is important to fully recognize those who have been marginalized in the church.

# Physicality, pleasure and freedom: a new look at God's creation

For a long time, church tradition tended to view *physicality and sensual pleasure* as a threatening counterweight to the spiritual. From St. Augustine until well into the modern era, Catholic thinking was characterized by the idea that sexual lust had to be curbed or even fought against in order to grow spiritually. However, this thinking is increasingly at odds with a holistic Christian view of humanity. The biblical message of creation says: *"God looked at everything he had made: it was very good."* This also includes the body with its urges and pleasures. Physicality is not a lower sphere to be overcome, but part of the God-given identity of human beings. The doctrine of God becoming man (incarnation) in particular emphasizes that God himself took on a human body in Jesus Christ, ate, drank - and presumably also shared the entire range of human emotions and sensual pleasures. This central Christian mystery ennobles the body and the bodily experience. A sexual morality in the spirit of the incarnation would not see the body as the enemy of the soul, but as its expression and *"temple of the Holy Spirit"* (1 Cor 6:19).

This goes hand in hand with a more positive view of pleasure. Lust in sexuality - understood as the joy of tenderness, excitement and physical oneness - can have something sacred in a loving relationship. Where two people give themselves to each other in love, lust can be seen as a *gift from God*, not as the work of the devil. The times when the church only associated lust with sin are over: Today, we speak more of responsible lust. It is about integrating sexual desire into personality and relationships. It is not the suppression of lust that leads to a moral life, but the mature handling of it. It is emphasized, for example, that true *ethical maturity* is shown in how a person deals freely and responsibly with their physicality - out of love and insight, not out of blind obedience. This maturity means that one neither demonizes one's own urges nor is at the mercy of them without restraint, but brings them into harmony with higher values. So instead of seeing lust as a danger to the soul, it can be understood as a force that finds its rightful place in committed love.

Finally, there is freedom, which is central to Christian ethics. *"For freedom Christ has set us free"* (Gal 5:1) - these words of St. Paul also apply to the area of sexuality. God does not want underage children who follow rules without understanding them. Rather, every believer should grow into the freedom of God's children, which means making decisions - including ethical ones - in their own conscience before God. Catholic moral teaching recognizes the principle of the primacy of conscience , according to which the personal conscience is the ultimately binding authority in moral questions. Of course, the conscience needs education and guidance, but ultimately an adult can only act morally if they do so *freely* and out of conviction. A sexual ethic that takes self-determination seriously trusts that responsible Christians are able to live their sexuality in a way that does not harm anyone, but promotes love and life. Obedience out of fear of punishment takes a back seat to this. This does not mean arbitrariness - responsibility and commitment to the values of the Gospel remain the standard - but it does mean that the final decision is made in dialog between the individual and God, not through external coercion.

## On the way to a pro-life sexual morality for the 21st century

The question *"Is Catholic sexual morality beneficial or distant from life?"* can probably only be answered dialectically in the present day: In its previous, rigid form, it was for many rather distant from life, even hostile to life - but in its renewed form it could actually have a beneficial effect on life. The church is at a turning point. A growing number of believers, theologians and even bishops are recognizing that the traditional doctrines on sexuality need to be rethought so that they no longer *become a stumbling block* for people, but rather *a guide* once again. The basic direction of this new sexual ethic is clear: responsibility, love and self-determination have priority over mere obedience to traditional norms. This means a morality that no longer brands every breach of a rule as a serious sin, but looks at the whole of personality and relationship. It also means respecting the voice of each individual's conscience - in the confidence that the Holy Spirit is at work in believers and wants to lead them to a life of fullness.

A pro-life sexual morality in the 21st century would be an ethic of *relationship and integrity*. It would encourage couples - whether married or not, homosexual or heterosexual - to shape their sexuality responsibly and lovingly. It would offer criteria for what responsible means: for example, fidelity and reliability instead of selfishness, consensuality and respect instead of assault, sincere communication instead of concealment. Such criteria appeal to laypeople and clergy alike and take account of what many are already living. This would not abolish church teaching, but rather deepen it in the light of the Gospel: Jesus said few words about sexual morality, but all the more about love, mercy and truthfulness. Every morality must be measured against this.

At present, many believers experience the official teaching as a burden, not as guidance. It does not lead to more faithfulness, but to more silence, shame and turning away. This must change - not out of adaptation to the spirit of the times, but out of faithfulness to the Spirit of God, who does not hold people down, but lifts them up.

## Four basic principles of a life-serving sexual morality

A pro-life sexual morality should be based on four basic principles:

1.  **Love** - as the reason for the relationship,
2.  **Responsibility** - as a benchmark for action,
3.  **Self-determination** - as an expression of maturity,
4.  **Devotion** - as a theological standard: *"Where there is love, there is God."*

A life-serving sexual morality is based on an attitude that affirms, promotes and respects life in all its diversity. At its core, it is based on four central principles that are interwoven and complement each other:

The first and most fundamental principle is **love as the foundation of every relationship**. This love is far more than a romantic feeling; rather, it means the deep, caring and sincere devotion of which the apostle Paul speaks in First Corinthians: *"Now faith, hope and love remain, these three; but love is the greatest of these."* (1 Cor 13:13). Love as the basis of a relationship is expressed in mutual respect, trust and appreciation - regardless of external standards or conventional expectations.

The second principle is **responsibility as a yardstick for action**. Responsible sexuality recognizes the consequences of one's own actions and takes care of others and oneself. Taking responsibility means never viewing the other person merely as a means of satisfying one's own needs, but perceiving them as a valuable counterpart whose dignity is to be respected at all times. Galatians 6:2 says: *"Bear one another's burdens, and in this way you will fulfill the law of Christ."* Responsibility in sexuality therefore manifests itself in an attitude that bears burdens together and seeks solutions together that do justice to both people in the relationship.

Thirdly, a pro-life sexual morality absolutely needs the principle of **self-determination as an expression of personal maturity**. Every person should be free to take control of their own life and make sovereign decisions about themselves. A mature, responsible person consciously takes responsibility for their decisions and equally respects the autonomy of others. The apostle Paul emphasizes in his letter to the Galatians: *"Christ has set us free!"* (Gal 5:1). In the modern age, this principle is reflected in the fact that people today are increasingly insisting on their right to decide freely about partnership, family planning and their own sexual orientation without having to experience pressure or paternalism from society, church or state.

Finally, the fourth and theologically most profound principle is **devotion as a theological standard**. This principle is based on the deep conviction that God is present wherever there is true love and living devotion. For, as the first letter of John puts it: *"God is love, and he who abides in love abides in God and God in him."* (1 John 4:16). This perspective calls for sexuality not to be viewed primarily as a field to be morally regulated, but as a space in which God can be experienced - provided that sexuality is lived out of honest, caring and deep connection.

*Figure 12 : The four basic principles of the life-serving sexual morality of a new church: love, responsibility, self-determination and care for others.*

*A minimalist and symbolic infographic on a yellow background, depicting a cycle of four clear symbols: A red heart (for love), a head with an arrow pointing upwards (for personal development or awareness), a hand with a shield (for protection and safety) and a hand with a cross (for faith and spirituality). The symbols are connected by lines and form a closed circle. Ideal for depicting themes relating to love, personal and spiritual development as well as security and safety in faith contexts in order to discuss a life-serving sexual morality of the Catholic Church.*

A modern example in which these principles become visible is the way many churches deal with same-sex partnerships today. More and more Christian communities are recognizing that God is alive and at work in a loving, responsible, self-determined and committed partnership - regardless of gender or orientation. Initiatives such as *"Out in Church"* or movements such as *"Maria 2.0"* clearly advocate placing these life-serving sexual ethics at the center of church teaching and practice. In this way, they contribute to the church and society opening up in equal measure and recognizing the beauty, dignity and closeness to God of the diversity of love and life plans.

If the church learns this language, it could reach more people again - not through rules, but through *resonance*. A *theology of resonance* is needed in the question of sexual morality.

The implementation of this or a renewed sexual ethic is a process that requires time, dialog and courageous decisions. Documents such as *Amoris laetitia* (2016) have cautiously opened doors by emphasizing that no one should be condemned forever and that the *logic of mercy* also applies to questions of family and sexuality. The worldwide synodal process of the Church initiated by Pope Francis also shows that these topics are on the agenda . Creating awareness for humane and spiritually responsible sexual ethics is the order of the day. Ultimately, nothing less is at stake than the credibility of the Church and its mission to serve people on their journey through life in the light of the Gospel.

The vision is of a church that rejoices with people when love succeeds instead of just keeping a record of sins; a church that accompanies rather than condemns in matters of sexuality, thereby making the liberating core of Christ's message tangible anew. Such a sexual morality would actually *be beneficial to life*: it would do justice to people's lives, strengthen relationships, heal wounds and celebrate the deep joy and responsibility that lie in the gift of sexuality. There is a long way to go: towards a *pro-life theology* - but the steps have begun, and many believers are already taking them today, in the hope of a church that places love above all else.

*What the church needs is not greater sexual control - but a deeper capacity for love.*

# Chapter 9:
# Can God also be thought of as queer? - Theological tradition and diversity in the image of God

*The chapter is dedicated to the question of whether God can also be thought of as "queer" - and which sexual orientations he could then have in principle - and thus questions the traditional male-dominated image of God. The Christian tradition is often dominated by a patriarchal understanding of God as Father, Lord or King, which is closely linked to social power structures and thus religiously legitimizes male dominance. Ultimately, God is united with the incarnate Jesus Christ. Feminist and queer theological perspectives offer significant alternatives to this by pointing out that biblical representations of God are already diverse and contain both female and non-binary metaphors. For example, passages from Isaiah or Deuteronomy show God with maternal and childbearing aspects. Wisdom (Sophia) appears in the Bible as a female and combines male and female attributes of God. Queer theology goes further and argues that God's being transcends all binary gender categories and has a dynamic, diverse and inclusive (and loving) identity. Art and philosophy support this approach by depicting God's infinity creatively and diversely, thus engaging people of all genders and identities spiritually. In liturgy and catechesis, there are also initial attempts to put inclusive and diverse images of God into practice.*

- *Question: How can traditional Christian communities expand their image of God to better reflect the diversity and complexity of human experience and authentically capture God's essence beyond patriarchal and binary notions?*
- *Question: Isn't a church that strictly adheres to a patriarchal image of God ultimately partly responsible for the exclusion and*

discrimination of all those people whose reality of life does not fit into a binary or heteronormative scheme?

- **Option for action:** The Catholic Church should officially revise its liturgical texts, prayers and catechism materials in order to formulate images of God in a gender-equitable and diverse way and thus actively enable an inclusive, lively and authentic relationship with God for all believers.

- **Training option:** Clergy, believers and pupils in religious education should acquire skills in feminist and queer theology, gender-sensitive language and intercultural sensitivity through targeted training and workshops in order to reflect on traditional images of God, shape them in a diversity-conscious way and credibly implement this theological expansion in everyday life and church life. It is also about learning to decode the various sexual orientations in terms of LGBTQIA+ and what is associated with them.

In the Christian tradition, God is often addressed with male titles and images - as Father, Lord or King. This one-sided male image of God reflects historical patriarchal structures and has long shaped theology and liturgy. The feminist theologian Mary Daly put it succinctly: *"If God is male, the male is God.*

In doing so, she addressed the fact that an exclusively male image of God sacralizes male supremacy and excludes women from divine symbolism. Such an understanding has an impact on the community: As long as a male-patriarchal image of God dominates the symbolic order of the church, true equality remains difficult.

Modern theologians, on the other hand, emphasize that our talk about God can only ever be approximate and that God transcends all our ideas.

Precisely because God *is "greater than can be conceived"* (Anselm of Canterbury), this opens up a variety of images and ways of expression.

Tradition and dogma therefore do not have to remain fixed to one gender image - on the contrary, diverse images of God can better appreciate God's infinity.

## Biblical images of God beyond the masculine

The Bible itself offers plenty of material for female and non-binary images of God.

Although male forms of address predominate, in many places God appears in female, maternal or gender-independent metaphors:

- **God as a comforting mother:** *"As a mother comforts her son, so I comfort you"* - this is what God says in Isaiah 66:13.

In Isaiah 49:15, God also compares his love to the unforgettable love of a mother. Jesus himself uses a feminine image for his divine concern in Matthew 23:37, comparing himself to a hen who wants to gather her chicks under her wings. This imagery emphasizes God's care and closeness in a motherly way.

Figure13 : Drawing of a queer-friendly figure.

*A friendly and modern illustration of a figure in a minimalist illustrator's style. She raises her right hand in blessing, while her left hand rests gently on his chest. A striking rainbow halo surrounds the head, conveying a symbolic message of love, diversity and acceptance. The image is ideal for content around LGBTQIA+-friendly theology, inclusive spirituality and religious openness - also to artistically discuss divine and/or queer characteristics of, for example, the incarnate God Jesus Christ.*

- **God as the one who gives birth:** In the Old Testament, there is even explicit birthing language for God. In Deuteronomy 32:18 it says: *"You* have *forsaken the rock that brought you forth; you have forgotten the God who gave you birth."* Here, both paternal (generating) and maternal (giving birth) aspects of God are mentioned in a single verse.

The combination of these images shows that God is not limited to one gender, but unites gender diversity in himself.

In other words, even the "God-He" of the Bible can have typically female and typically male attributes at the same time - there is a certain *fluidity of the gender dimension* in the Old Testament representations of God.

- **Wisdom (Sophia) as a female manifestation of God:** In the Judeo-Christian wisdom tradition, God's wisdom appears in a female form. Thus *Chokhmah* (Hebrew) or *Sophia* (Greek) is personified in Proverbs 8, or in late writings such as the wisdom literature (Wisdom 7), as a woman who works alongside God. In the New Testament, Christ is referred to as the *"wisdom of God"* (1 Cor 1:24), which builds a bridge between *the male* and female representation of God.

This juxtaposition - female wisdom and male Christ - *"reveals a divine fluidity that cannot be pinned down to a single gender identity or a one-sided relationship."*

The Holy Spirit is also referred to in Hebrew with the feminine word *Ruach*; some Christian traditions therefore emphasize the feminine traits of the Spirit.

- **God beyond grammatical gender categories:** When Moses asks God for *his* name, God responds with *"I am who I am"* (Exodus 3:14). Interestingly, this self-revelation in Hebrew is formulated in a gender-neutral way.

The name of God *YHWH* also has no grammatical gender marker. This indicates that God exists beyond human categories of *male* and *female*.

In the New Testament, Paul abolishes social gender boundaries in Galatians 3:28: *"There is no longer male or female, for you are all one in Christ Jesus."* If male and female are not separated in salvation in

Christ, this reflects the fact that God himself is also above such dichotomies.

In summary, biblical revelation transcends the one-dimensional male concept of God. From creation (in which humans are created *"as man and woman"* in the image of God) to maternal images and cross-gender statements, the Bible shows a God who unites diverse (gender) aspects and cannot be reduced to a single category.

This biblical basis also legitimizes diverse images of God theologically. As Pope John Paul I once surprisingly put it: *"God is Father, but even more he is Mother"* - a statement that encourages us to think of God beyond restrictive norms.

## Feminist theology: criticism of the patriarchal image of God

Since the 1960s, feminist theology has been a major theme of the dominant male concept of God and has pointed out alternatives. Mary Daly - a pioneer of this movement - pointed out that the insistent image of *God as male* served to oppress women by presenting male dominance as God-ordained. Her famous dictum *"If God is masculine, the masculine is God"* sums up how religious language reflects power relations. Daly therefore called for a radical rethinking of the concept of God - beyond patriarchal categories - or to break away from a patriarchal religious system altogether.

Other feminist theologians have endeavored to make the female dimension of God visible again without abandoning Christianity. Elisabeth Schüssler Fiorenza, for example, reconstructed the forgotten contributions of women in the early church in her work *In Memory of Her* (1983). She coined the approach of *"making the memory of women visible"*, which became fundamental for later feminist theologies.

Schüssler Fiorenza and others (e.g. Dorothee Sölle, Rosemary Radford Ruether, Elisabeth Moltmann-Wendel) showed that women have experienced and proclaimed God's closeness in the Bible and church history - but established theology has marginalized these testimonies. Feminist theology reveals how closely the image of God and power are linked: An exclusively male image of God legitimizes male domination, while diverse images of God encourage equality and inclusion.

Feminist theologians therefore suggest that God should also be addressed in female metaphors - for example as a mother, a woman giving birth, wisdom or a "goddess". The Catholic theologian Leonardo Boff (inspired by liberation theology) spoke of the *"motherliness of God"*; in *Models of God*, the Protestant theologian Sallie McFague developed new metaphors (God as mother, lover, friend) to complement the father-son schema. Elizabeth A. Johnson emphasized with the title *She Who Is* that God's being can also be called feminine . Such approaches are theologically sound: If *men and women* are created equally in the image of God, then the image of God itself must include a fullness. Feminist theology reminds us that talking about God was never a purely male affair - many biblical women (from Miriam to Hannah to Mary) proclaimed God's word. These insights pave the way for thinking and addressing God in theology *in a gender-equitable* way.

## Queer theological perspectives: God beyond binary genders

While feminist theology initially emphasized the feminine side of God, queer theology goes one step further. It asks whether God is fundamentally transcendent of our gender categories - i.e. neither male nor female, but *"queer" in the sense of different* and outside binary norms. Queer theology ties in with the fact that God's nature and love are not bound to human norms: God breaks down all pigeonholes, be it in terms of gender, sexuality or relationship patterns.

In her book *The Queer God* (2003), Argentinian theologian Marcella Althaus-Reid speaks explicitly of a "queer God". In it, she "queers" the entire classical doctrine of God by consistently questioning why God should be bound to heteronormativity in thought and representation.

Althaus-Reid effectively demonstrates that even the biblical message - such as Jesus' treatment of the marginalized - reveals a God who transcends the usual boundaries of purity and norms. Patrick S. Cheng, another queer theologian, describes God's love as *"radical love"*, a radical love that transcends all sexual and gender boundaries. In such a view, Christ is understood as the incarnation of this boundary-breaking love - as someone who broke through social norms (including gender norms) in order to accept all people.

Queer theology emphasizes that terms such as *male* and *female* are ultimately too narrow for the one who created heaven and earth. Instead, God's identity is understood as dynamic and relational . Some queer theological concepts even play with terms such as *"God is trans"* - not in the sense of a modern gender identity, but to express that God is *transcendent and transgressive* at the same time, beyond fixed roles. For example, an art installation in New York entitled *"God is Trans: A Queer Spiritual Journey"* showed God's proximity to trans* and queer experiences, which sparked both controversy and enthusiasm.

Such perspectives understand God's incarnation in Jesus Christ as a divine act of transgression: God transcended the boundary between Creator and creature - why shouldn't God also transcend the gender boundaries drawn by humans?

In theopoetics and queer-spiritual literature, God is celebrated in new images: as a dancing deity, as a loving being without pronouns, as goddess and god at the same time, even as a polyphonic counterpart that harmonizes all voices and identities within itself. These poetic approximations express what classical doctrines such as the Trinity imply: in God, relationship exists in diversity. The Trinity can be understood as a *"threefold love relationship in God"*, a model for non-exclusive, diverse love.

Some queer theologians even interpret God's love as polyamorous in the sense that God has many loving relationships with people without being exclusively committed to a single one.

All of these are figurative attempts to do justice to the boundless, queer dimension of God.

What is important is that thinking of God as queer does not mean imposing some modern label on God, but rather recognizing that God is by definition *"other"* - the completely different one who does not fit into our orders. If human gender identity can be fluid and socially constructed, as philosophers such as Judith Butler or Paul B. Preciado have shown, then God's identity should not be reduced to a gender cliché. Rather, God's nature can be understood as infinitely diverse - open to what lies beyond our norm. Queer theology invites us to break down the boundaries in our image of God. It reminds us that *"neither male nor female"* in God means lack, but fullness: God's love encompasses *all* forms of being and loving.

# Father, Son, Holy Spirit - and yet more than male

A frequent counter-argument against overly "queer" concepts of God is the traditional image of the Trinity. In Christianity, God reveals himself as Father, Son and Holy Spirit - two of these persons are clearly named as male, and Jesus, as a human being, was male. Does this not mean that God must be thought of as "male"? It is worth taking a closer look here. First of all, the term *Father* for God is an image that Jesus used to express God's loving authority and the origin of all life.

However, Jesus himself also speaks of God's maternal side, for example in parables that juxtapose male and female everyday scenes (e.g. the good shepherd and the searching woman with the lost drachma in Luke 15).

In Jesus Christ, the *Son* actually became a man - but the eternal Word of God, the Logos, eludes human gender categories. The second person of the Trinity has no biological gender beyond the incarnation. And the Holy Spirit? In many languages, "spirit" is neutral or feminine; the Bible uses images such as wind, fire or dove for the Spirit of God - all things without gender.

The Trinitarian concept of God is therefore not to be understood as a "purely male trio". Rather, the Trinity emphasizes that God is a *relationship*: Father, Son and Spirit are in loving communion. This inner relational event of God can certainly be interpreted in such a way that God already unites diversity and unity in himself - which some theologians even understand as a *model for a non-exclusive, diverse love*.

Swedish Archbishop Antje Jackelén, under whose leadership the Lutheran Church of Sweden introduced more gender-appropriate language for God in 2017, explains this as follows: *"We know from* theology that God is beyond our human gender distinction. *God is not a human being."*

God as the Triune One transcends the human and therefore also the male/female division. This is why many theologians do not see it as a falsification, but rather as a complement to address God with female titles - as long as the relationship is preserved. For example, there are attempts to also call the first person of the Trinity "Mother" in prayer without denying God's fatherhood. After all, "father" is not a biological term here, but an expression of origin and love - including a maternal love of God can even deepen this meaning.

Opponents of such changes, however, warn of a break with tradition: one theologian in Sweden even said that addressing God too neutrally would undermine the doctrine of the Trinity and alienate the church from its common heritage. However, the Trinity also means that if God became incarnate in Jesus Christ and he had a sexual orientation as a human being, then it must also be possible in principle to attribute this to God - this applies not only to the category of gender, but also in principle to sexual feelings with this gender.

However, these theses and concerns overlook the fact that the Church has always found new images to describe the mystery of God without destroying the dogma of faith. As Bishop Franz Jung emphasizes, we must not make a single image absolute - *"it becomes dangerous when an image [...] becomes absolute"*.

The father-son language remains central, but it does not exclude other perspectives. On the contrary: if we emphasize that God is more than a human father, then maternal or cross-gender images can help to express this *surplus*. It remains important - as taught by the Fourth Lateran Council - that with every metaphor of God we also bear in mind that God is completely different - and therefore queer - and greater than our imagination.

In this way, God can also be encountered in the imagination as a "young black woman" - as Bishop Jung says: "She may not be God himself, *but God can meet me in her.*

This shows: The doctrine of the Trinity does not want to fix God forever as an old white man, but to lead us into a relationship with a living God who transcends all our images.

# Extra-church impulses: gender studies, queer philosophy and art

Impulses for expanded images of God come not only from theology itself, but also from thinkers outside the church - for example from gender studies, queer philosophy or art. Feminist poet Audre Lorde, for example, has emphasized the spiritual power of female identity: In her essay *"The Uses of the Erotic"*, she describes the erotic (not in the banal sense, but as the deepest life energy) as lying on a *"deeply feminine and spiritual level"*. Lorde's message - that real power and creativity comes from recognizing the feminine and other within us - can also be applied to concepts of God. It implies: A spiritual conception that only honors masculinity gives away a source of divine power. For Lorde, differences (be it in gender, skin color, sexuality) are *sacred*, not flaws. This way of thinking encourages us to seek God in people's diverse experiences - for example, in the experience of a black lesbian woman as well as in that of a white heterosexual man. God reveals himself in the fullness of life, not just in a standard type.

The philosopher Judith Butler has shown that gender is a *"performative"* construct - it is formed by the repetition of roles, not by a static being. If we reflexively apply this understanding to religion, we realize that the idea that "God is a he (man)" is ultimately also a performance, a traditionally repeated attribution that should not be confused with a divine reality. Butler's gender theory encourages theologians to speak of God in deconstructed categories. If language and role models can be changed, God's language can also be changed so as not to unintentionally cement oppression . Queer philosophy in general - for example with thinkers such as Paul B. Preciado or Donna Haraway - explodes the idea of fixed identities. Applied to the question of God, this means that perhaps we should speak of *relationship* and *diversity* rather than identity. God would then be the network of relationships that connects everything, the one who appears in plurality (cf. Haraway's idea of deity as a network).

In art, the question *"What does God look like?"* has long been answered creatively. Artists have depicted God as a woman, as an androgyne, as many-faced. In multi-religious art projects - e.g. exhibitions in which painters from different religions show their ideas of God - the divine sometimes appears as Mother Earth, sometimes as a being of light without gender, sometimes with changing figures. Such images can inspire people of faith to overcome their own narrowness of thought. A more recent example from popular culture: in some series or films (such as *"The Shack"*), God is shown beyond stereotypical images - here, for example, God appears as a warm-hearted black woman, Jesus as an approachable man and the Holy Spirit as a wise Asian woman. This creative freedom shows that our concept of God does not have to be static. Interfaith dialogs can also provide impulses: The experience of the Hindu idea that the divine knows both male and female figures (such as Shiva and Shakti), or the indigenous idea of a two-gendered creator being, can help Christians to think of their own God more richly (without giving up the uniqueness of God).

Civil society initiatives are also contributing to the debate: For example, the Catholic Student Youth (KSJ) launched a campaign in 2020 to write God with a gender asterisk as *"God:"*. The aim was to make it clear that God does not have to be an old white man with a beard, but that the image of God and language should be inclusive.

The sometimes heated reactions to this - from enthusiastic approval to fierce rejection - show how much the image of God remains a controversial topic. But they also show that when young people ask for a contemporary image of God, they not only encounter resistance, but also lively interest.

The public debate about whether it is permissible to address God as "Father and Mother", whether a gender asterisk in "God*" / "God:" makes sense, or whether Jesus was perhaps queer, is forcing theology and the church to take a stand. As a result, thought-provoking impulses from outside the church flow into the church's self-reflection - a salutary process to break up encrusted ideas.

# Diverse images of God in liturgy and catechesis

How do inclusive images of God affect liturgy, prayer and catechesis in concrete terms? Theological insights into diversity and gender equality only unfold their power when they are actually implemented in church life. For several decades now, congregations - mainly Protestant, but increasingly also Catholic - have been experimenting with gender-inclusive language for God. For example, prayers use phrases such as *"God, you mother and father at the same time..."* or deliberately switch between "God" and "Goddess". In feminist women's liturgies, God is invoked as Mother or with the name "Sophia", which emphasizes the feminine aspect of divine wisdom.

An interesting example of this is the move by the Church of Sweden, which officially recommended that male pronouns for God should be avoided in church services wherever possible. Instead of "He" or "Lord", simply "God" should be used so as not to suggest a one-sided gender attribution. This decision was the result of a long discussion process that led to the adaptation of their liturgical handbook in 2017. The Protestant Church in Switzerland has now also developed official guidelines that explicitly recommend inclusive language forms.

The Catholic Church is also slowly moving on the subject. Official prayer texts are only changing cautiously, as the missals are prescribed by the Vatican, but there are still cautious steps being taken here too: Pope Francis himself spoke publicly about the *"maternal tenderness of God"*, thus legitimizing developments that are already taking place at grassroots level. Some Catholic parishes are trying out creative new addresses to God, particularly at youth services or special blessings - e.g. *"God, the source of all life - father and mother of creation"*.

One concrete example of gender-equitable liturgy in the Catholic context is the blog "Gotteswort, weiblich" (Word of God, female), which was created in the diocese of Aachen in 2019. The initiator, a women's pastoral worker, is convinced that an inclusive liturgical language is essential for true gender equality in the church. Every Sunday, biblical interpretations, intercessions or blessing texts are published there that consciously integrate female images of God such as "loving mother" or "the Eternal". The response is clear: many believers feel personally addressed and included.

In church education work, especially in catechesis for children and young people, there is also an expansion of the image of God. Modern religion books and materials encourage young people to discover God in a variety of images - as father, mother, friend, light or power. Children are allowed to draw or creatively describe God without fixed answers. The results are varied and colorful: God appears as a woman with long hair, a shining sun or an abstract force such as a heart and a whirlwind. Theologians such as Martina Bär emphasize this approach and encourage us to consciously convey God as both a mother and a father. Catechists report that children are often more open to this expanded idea of God than adults, who cling to the traditional image of the old man with a beard.

Inclusive images of God are also becoming increasingly common in church music. New hymns explicitly sing about God with female attributes (*"God is like a mother who never forgets her child..."*). Intercessions are increasingly saying: "*You God with a motherly heart...*".

Special church services such as ecumenical CSD services send a particularly strong signal of inclusion. They feature creative wordplay and banners such as *"God is transcendent"* to make it clear that God transcends all gender boundaries. These inclusive forms of language in prayer and liturgy are not intended to encourage anyone to reflect, but rather to make the infinite breadth and diversity of God tangible in language - and thus open our hearts to the liberating message of divine love. Where space is created for new images of God, people often experience for the first time the depth of a love that imposes no conditions.

# Outlook: Allowing God's infinity and taking diversity seriously

The question of whether God can be conceived queerly leads us to a fundamental theological insight: God is ultimately unavailable and transcends any human conception. God's infinity means that no single image or word can be sufficient to grasp God's reality. If we take this unavailability of God seriously, then this means not only allowing diversity in our images of God, but actively promoting it. Every generation and every culture must search anew for images that make God's presence tangible, while recognizing that God always remains bigger and different than we think.

Diversity in speaking of God is therefore not confusion, but an expression of a profound truth: God eludes final definition. Biblical and theological traditions offer us many different metaphors for this: God as father and mother, friend and girlfriend, as bridegroom and bride, as protector and comforter, power, light, fire or dance. None of these metaphors is sufficient on its own, but all of them together open our eyes to God's all-encompassing presence and love. Queer and feminist theologies remind us of what should actually be self-evident: God is not male, not female, but transcendent, beyond gender boundaries. Thinking God queer therefore does not mean following a fashion, but seriously recognizing that God's reality transcends all human categories.

This openness to queer and inclusive images of God has practical consequences for church practice. Liturgy, prayers and sermons should consciously create space for diverse images of God. For example, phrases such as *"God, who is father and mother"* or *"source of all life"* could be used in intercessions or hymns. At the same time, the congregation should always be invited to address God in silent prayer with their own personal images. This does not take away anyone's familiar image, but makes it clear how much bigger and closer God can actually be.

It is precisely the inclusive speech of God that helps people who feel marginalized or hurt by traditional images - for example women, LGBTQIA+ people or men who struggle with a harsh image of the father

187

- to find new approaches to God. Such diverse images of God enable a church that is free from shame, guilt and exclusion. The church becomes a space in which differences are not experienced as a threat, but as an enrichment. In this atmosphere of openness, people can experience that God's love is unconditional and welcomes every form of identity.

A *theology of diversity* explicitly emphasizes that all people are created in the image of God. The colorful diversity of human identities - whether male, female, trans*, inter* or non-binary - reflects in its own way the boundless diversity of God. In this respect, opening up to queer and diverse images of God is not only legitimate, but a necessary step in order to do justice to the message of the Gospel. Jesus Christ broke religious taboos and explicitly placed marginalized people at the center. In the spirit of Jesus, the church today can overcome rigid and limiting images of God without abandoning its tradition.

Thinking of God in new, queer and feminist images therefore does not mean a loss, but rather a gain in depth, truth and closeness to the God who is present in everything and wants to be "all in all". It is precisely this that shows that we take God's mystery seriously: An image of God that is too narrow could easily become an idol - a God that we create according to our own standards. However, the God of the Bible and the Christian tradition transcends all boundaries. Let us therefore take God's infinite diversity seriously and allow ourselves to be constantly surprised anew by the God whose love is radically inclusive and truly queer - because it transcends all norms and boundaries and welcomes all people without conditions.

# Chapter 10:
# What does Christian truth mean in interfaith dialog?

*The chapter deals with the question of what Christian truth means in interreligious dialog. The starting point is the theologian Hans Küng's idea that world peace is only possible when there is peace between religions, and that this peace can only be achieved through open dialog. Christian truth is not an absolute possession, but a truth lived in relationship, which humbly acknowledges that no one possesses the entire divine truth. Central to this is the idea of God's incarnation in Jesus Christ, who reveals truth as lived love and humility. The Second Vatican Council and subsequent popes have taken significant steps towards an attitude that recognizes and values non-Christian religions without giving up one's own faith identity. Pope Francis emphasizes in particular that interreligious dialogue is not relativistic, but an expression of the fraternal search for truth. Dialogue practice in concrete projects, such as the House of One in Berlin, the Interfaith Gender Justice Network in South Africa or the Queer Interfaith Coalition in Toronto, illustrates how common values such as peace, justice and human dignity can also have a unifying effect on controversial issues such as gender justice and LGBTQIA+ rights. Christian truth in dialog thus proves to be alive and adaptive, oriented towards the dignity of all people.*

- **Question:** *How can faith in Jesus Christ be lived as "the truth" without simultaneously devaluing or marginalizing the truth content and spiritual depth of other religions?*
- **Question:** *Is it possible for a Christian to represent faith in Christ as the only way to God and at the same time recognize that God can reveal himself equally authentically in other religions without this relativizing his own faith?*
- **Option for action:** *The Catholic Church should establish regular interreligious councils worldwide, in which representatives of*

*different faiths work together to develop binding statements on current issues of justice, human dignity and peace, in order to not only promote interreligious dialog in theory, but also to initiate concrete joint action.*

- ***Training option:** Clergy, believers and pupils should train skills such as intercultural and interreligious communication skills, empathy towards those who think differently and a reflective approach to their own faith identity in religious education lessons or in specific seminars. Workshops in which authentic encounters with members of other religions take place could serve this purpose, not only to impart knowledge about other religions, but also to reduce personal prejudices and to be able to represent one's own religious position humbly and clearly at the same time.*

*"No world peace without peace among the religions. No religious peace without dialog between the world's religions*

With these memorable theses, the theologian Hans Küng summed up why religious claims to absoluteness stand in the way of peace.

Those who consider their own religion to be absolute and devalue others make understanding more difficult and stir up conflict. But what does *Christian truth* mean in this context? Does believing in Jesus Christ as *"the way, the truth and the life"* (John 14:6) automatically mean that all other paths should be labeled as error? We need to shed light on how the Christian concept of truth and interreligious dialog can come together - in a spirit of humility, incarnation and lived love. It must be shown how firm conviction can succeed without claiming absoluteness, what impulses the Second Vatican Council and Pope Francis provide, what common values are in the foreground and how concrete interreligious initiatives - for example in Berlin, South Africa and Toronto - make opportunities for dialog visible. The end result must be a call for a *theology of diversity* that seeks truth in relationship rather than in demarcation.

## Humility and Incarnation: The Christian concept of truth

In Christianity, truth is not simply a collection of dogmas, but first and foremost a person: Jesus Christ. *"The Word became flesh"* - God's eternal truth becomes man in Jesus (John 1:14). This incarnation reveals a core of Christian truth: humility. God reveals the truth not as a shattering bolt from above, but as a vulnerable child in a manger and as a servant Messiah who washes the disciples' feet. For Christians, this means that truth goes hand in hand with love and humility. Anyone who claims to *possess* the whole truth fails to recognize the greatness of God. *"Now through a mirror we see only mysterious outlines... but then face to face"* (1 Cor 13:12) - even believing Christians only ever see truth in fragments. This is why the Christian tradition urges humility: true knowledge of God does not lead to arrogance, but to amazement and respect for the mystery. For Jesus, lived love - charity, mercy, justice - is the standard of truth. The Gospel of John makes it clear that we should *"do the truth"* (John 3:21), i.e. live a life of love and sincerity. Christian truth is therefore *relational* and inclusive: it manifests itself in our relationship with God and our fellow human beings, not in self-opinionated isolation.

This theological insight lays the foundation for dialog: If God is love (1 John 4:8) and every person is made in the image of God, then the search for truth requires a respectful exchange with all people. An attitude of humility means recognizing that God is greater than our limited understanding. As the Ecumenical Patriarch Bartholomew once aptly put it: *"Truth is not afraid of dialog, because truth is never in danger from dialog."*

*Figure14 : Where is inter-religious dialog heading?*

*A minimalist depiction of four religious symbols in a row, black on a neutral beige background: a Christian cross, the Islamic crescent with star, the Buddhist Dharma wheel and the Jewish Star of David. The image symbolizes interfaith dialogue, religious diversity and harmony between different faith communities. Ideally suited for topics relating to tolerance, mutual understanding and intercultural exchange.*

Those who really trust that Christ is the truth need not shy away from dialog - on the contrary: in every sincere conversation, a *"ray of that truth which enlightens all men"* can shine forth.

Christian truth then does not manifest itself as rigid possessiveness, but as a dynamic process of understanding - in openness to the work of God, even outside our own boundaries.

## Conviction without absolutes: how can this be achieved?

Many believers ask themselves: If I am convinced that Jesus Christ is the Savior, how can I *not* make the claim of absoluteness? Does dialog mean a betrayal of the uniqueness of Christ? The answer lies in a differentiated love of truth. Christian faith confesses that the fullness of truth is present in Christ. Yet this truth is not a club to beat others down, but an invitation to all. Since the Second Vatican Council, the Church has explicitly taught that there is also *truth and holiness* in other religions. *"The Catholic Church does not reject anything that is true and holy in these religions,"* it says in *Nostra aetate*.

Everything that is truly good, holy and righteous - in whatever tradition - has its ultimate origin in God. Christians can therefore rejoice in the wisdom and virtue that they discover in other faith communities instead of rejecting them.

Religious conviction without a claim to absoluteness is achieved by distinguishing between *possessing the truth* and *standing in the truth*. No human being *possesses* God's truth completely - we are seekers. But we can live in the truth as far as God gives it to us and remain open to further understanding. In a conversation with young people, Pope Francis emphasized that a dialogue cannot begin by presenting one's own religion as superior: *"If we start the conversation with: 'My religion is the only true one, yours is false...' - where does that lead?"* he asked. The answer from a young woman was: "To ruin." Francis agreed and added: *"All religions are paths to God. They are - to use a simile - like different languages that express the divine. But God is for everyone, and we are all God's children... There is only one God, and religions are like different languages, paths to reach God."*

This much-noticed comparison by the Pope does not mean that all differences are irrelevant, but that no one can "rent God for themselves". Every religion is like a language - none alone can express the whole word of God. Therefore, translation work and dialog are needed. For committed Christians, this means being firmly rooted in their own faith and at the same time open to what God wants to say to them through the testimony of others. This creates a faith that combines clarity and humility.

Patriarch Bartholomew of Constantinople put it this way from an Orthodox perspective: *"Those who believe that (their own) Orthodoxy has the truth are not afraid of dialog, because truth has never been threatened by dialog."*

Similarly, Christians trust that Christ as personified truth is not diminished when speaking with people of other faiths. On the contrary - in the encounter you can rediscover the depth of your own truth, free from false fear and fanaticism. Claims to absoluteness no longer apply when you realize that God is the absolute source of truth, not my human version of it. In this way, you can confess that *"Christ is the way and the truth for me"* and still allow others to find their way to God. The maxim is: *truth without love is hard, love without truth is arbitrary.* In interreligious coexistence, Christians are called to bear witness to *"the truth in love"* (cf. Eph 4:15) - confidently, but never certain that their own image is an absolute one.

# From the Second Vatican Council to Pope Francis: opening up to dialog

The Second Vatican Council (1962-65) marked a turning point in the attitude of the churches towards other religions. In the declaration *Nostra aetate*, the Catholic bishops explicitly acknowledged their appreciation of non-Christian faiths for the first time. They acknowledged that all peoples are in search of answers to the ultimate questions and stated: *"With sincere seriousness she considers those ways of acting and living, those precepts and teachings (of other religions) which, while differing in many points from what she herself holds and teaches, nevertheless not infrequently reveal a ray of that truth which enlightens all men."*

Recognizing these *rays of truth* in other religions without relativizing Christ's own proclamation was a new balance. On the one hand, the Church affirmed its mission to proclaim Christ as the fullness of revelation, but at the same time emphasized the commonalities: the common origin of all people in God and the common goal, God's kingdom of peace.

Since then, the Catholic Church - and similarly many Protestant churches - has actively sought interreligious dialog. In 1986, Pope John Paul II invited representatives of all world religions to Assisi to pray for peace - a strong sign that praying *together* is more conducive to peace than fighting against each other. Although Pope Benedict XVI emphasized the unique truth of Christ, he continued the dialogue and visited synagogues and mosques.

Under Pope Francis, interreligious dialog is experiencing a new dawn in the spirit of fraternity. In 2019, Francis signed a *document on human brotherhood* together with the Grand Imam of Al-Azhar, which states that God wants reconciliation and unity among people of all religions. In 2021, he visited the Shiite Grand Ayatollah in Najaf (Iraq) and prayed in the Ur of the Chaldeans with representatives of various religions. Francis' theology is characterized by *dialogue, humility and mercy: "The depth of religious desire invites humility regarding our role in the divine plan,"* he explained. He warns against misusing religion for hatred and instead emphasizes the common pilgrimage of all people *"in search of God"*, which is based on mutual respect and love lived together. In a letter to the rabbi of Rome, Francis wrote that his wish was to continue on the path of friendly encounters - in continuation of the spirit of Vatican II.

Francis likes to use the image of building bridges: As *pontiff* ("bridge builder"), the Bishop of Rome is called to build bridges between God and people and between people themselves. Building bridges here means reaching out to others, listening, working *together* for justice and peace. *"You cannot forge true bonds with God by ignoring your fellow human beings,"* says Francis. Religion must never be used as a pretext for violence - *"you can never affirm the divine by destroying the human"*, he said, referring to fanaticism. Instead, he called for gentleness and meekness, which should not be confused with weakness: A religious leader can *"appear very strong and determined without exercising aggression"* - true leadership service is service to one's neighbor in love. This attitude of humility and service makes interreligious dialog fruitful from a Christian perspective: it is not about dominating the conversation, but about serving the truth together.

## Shared values: peace, justice, human dignity

At the heart of interfaith dialog are not abstract theories, but common values that all major religions share. These include, above all, respect for *human dignity*, the pursuit of *peace* and *justice* and the Golden Rule (*"Treat others as you would like them to treat you"*). In the 1990s, Hans

Küng and others initiated the *Global Ethic* Project, which formulated a minimal ethical consensus among religions - in essence: responsibility for each other and for one world. In fact, religious leaders repeatedly emphasize that love for one's neighbour has transcendental significance. *"Love your neighbor as yourself"* is not only found in the Bible, but also in all world religions.

Christians in particular, who believe in the Creator *of all* people, see every person as a creature of God. Christians can therefore *stand up together* with people of other faiths for what everyone has recognized as good: For the protection of life, for the poor, for reconciliation instead of war, for the integrity of creation. Pope Francis often emphasizes the culture of encounter: at a time when differences are often perceived as a threat, believers of different traditions should stand shoulder to shoulder when it comes to helping people in need or fighting injustice. This creates what he calls *"caravans of brotherhood and solidarity"*.

It is important that the dialog does not attempt to present the lowest common denominator as the new religion. It is *not* about leveling out all differences. Rather, the religions should use their own strength to point out the values that they share. For example, belief in the one God obliges Jews, Christians and Muslims to emphasize the unity of humanity; belief in the just God motivates us to work for justice ; belief in the merciful God calls us to be merciful ourselves. In this sense, the apostle Paul wrote: *"Whatever is true, whatever is noble, whatever is just, whatever is pure, whatever is lovely... be careful about these things"* (Phil 4:8) - such virtues are not limited to Christians. Interreligious dialog as a path to peace therefore means working together in *friendship* wherever possible. In the best case, there is even competition for the good: Each religion strives to realize peace and human love even more emphatically, not to outdo the other, but to raise the moral level of humanity together.

The *House of One* concept in Berlin is a practical example of emphasizing shared values. Here, Jews, Christians and Muslims are working together to build a house that combines a synagogue, church and mosque under one roof - including a central meeting space.

The idea behind it: The uniqueness of each religion is preserved (everyone has their own prayer rooms) and at the same time people meet daily under one roof. Differences are not denied, but are overshadowed by the shared *humanity and spirituality*. At House of One events, it became clear that all three Abrahamic religions emphasize, for example, the value of *justice* and *women's dignity* - even if they have different internal traditions. A workshop *on "Women in the religions"* made it clear how much the issue of gender roles affects believers. By bringing conservative and progressive voices into conversation, it became clear that every religion struggles for equality and justice - and that we can learn from each other. Shared values such as justice thus act as a bridge to openly discuss controversial topics such as the image of women or sexual ethics without immediately denying each other legitimacy.

## Dialogue in practice: Interfaith initiatives on difficult topics

Theory and theological explanations are one thing - but interreligious dialog proves itself *on the ground* in concrete initiatives. Three examples from different parts of the world show how religious diversity can be lived and how even sensitive issues such as sexual ethics and gender roles can be tackled together:

- **House of One (Berlin):** In the German capital, the unique idea of building a joint house of worship for Judaism, Christianity and Islam was born. In the *House of One*, a synagogue, a church and a mosque will be connected by a joint domed building.

Even before the building was completed, the associated foundation was already working on interfaith educational work. In 2022, Georgian Baptist Bishop Malkhaz Songulashvili received the *House of One Peace Prize* for his advocacy of tolerance.

Songulashvili has built a peace center in Tbilisi based on the House of One model, where a church, synagogue and mosque also coexist under one roof.

His commitment to those to be included is particularly noteworthy: *"He supports the LGBTQIA+ community in a country where this support can put one's own life at risk,"* said former Federal President Christian Wulff in praise of the award winner.

The House of One thus sets an example that solidarity with discriminated groups can be a common concern of religions. Women and men are also equally involved in the project itself; rabbis, pastors and Muslim theologians are committed to the house and openly address the role of women in their traditions. The initiative shows: Trust is built through *continuous cooperation*. People learn to respect differences, e.g. in liturgy or doctrine, *without losing sight of the common vision*: a peaceful coexistence of religions based on the dignity of every human being. The House of One thus becomes a *living parable* for the fact that Christian truth is not lost in dialog, but gains depth in cooperation with Judaism and Islam.

- **Interfaith Gender Justice Network (Southern Africa):** In South Africa and neighboring countries, Christian councils of churches have joined forces with other faith communities to form networks to promote gender justice and the protection of LGBTQIA+ people. One example is the *One Body* program initiated by the *Fellowship of Christian Councils in Southern Africa* in cooperation with the *Global Interfaith Network*. For several years now, pastors, priests and imams have been talking to LGBTQIA+ believers in safe spaces in order to reduce prejudice and violence.

In many of these dialogues, both sides experience a genuine exchange for the first time: for example, coordinator Lebohang Matela reported that both the clergy and the queer participants initially had "a distorted image of each other".

But by getting to know each other personally, something surprising happened: Pastors showed remorse for their ignorance and asked LGBTQIA+ people for forgiveness for the marginalization they had suffered.

Conversely, the sincere apology and the newly experienced compassion deeply touched the participants from the LGBTQIA+ community. In such moments, Matela says, both sides realize *"that they are all created in the image of God and are one body"* - hence the name of the project.

This interfaith network on gender justice has already initiated dialog processes in eight countries in southern Africa. Materials are jointly developed and used in the communities to promote a rethinking of sexuality and gender roles - always based on shared religious values such as compassion, justice and the sanctity of life.

The example shows impressively that interfaith dialog does not have to stop at difficult topics. On the contrary: dialog can open up *learning processes*, especially when it comes to controversial moral issues. Christian truth proves itself capable of dialog here - for example when church representatives realize that their traditional stance on homosexuality has contributed to violence and make corrections in the light of Christ's love.

- **LGBTQIA+ Dialogue Forum (Toronto):** Even in Western countries, where diversity is often part of everyday life, there are initiatives to bring *religious faith and sexual identity* into conversation. In Toronto, Canada, for example, a Queer Interfaith Coalition was recently established, bringing together over 100 leaders from more than 20 religious communities.

Their aim is to make *religious* voices heard that emphasize inclusion and human dignity. With the slogan *"Hate is not a religious value"*, they oppose the misuse of religion to justify homophobia. In June 2024, this alliance organized an *Interfaith Pride service* for the first time, at which queer people from different faith traditions prayed and celebrated together.

Such events send an important message: diversity is seen as enrichment and the spiritual gifts that each person - regardless of their sexual orientation - brings to the community are recognized. In a cosmopolitan city like Toronto, which is home to Christians, Jews, Muslims, Hindus, Sikhs, Buddhists and others, the Dialogue Forum creates a space where common positions can be developed. For example, they agreed on public statements against conversion "therapies" and against discrimination, supported by a broad religious alliance. Theologically, many draw on the basic idea that *God is love*. One rabbinical voice put it this way: *"If God is love and someone does not recognize the love of another person, they do not believe in God."*

This pointed quote shows how new insights grow in interreligious discourse: here, the old Christian insight *that "God is love"* is put to the test - by asking how a religious attitude that condemns loving relationships can be compatible with the God of love. In the Toronto Dialogue Forum, the participants confirm each other in the value that all love has in God's eyes. In this way, a climate is created in which even conservative believers can carefully get to know new perspectives without having to betray their faith. Such local initiatives, whether in Toronto or elsewhere, contribute to the theology of diversity being put into practice: Christian truth is not revealed here as a rigid doctrine, but as a living dialog in which *truthfulness* and *love for one's neighbour* come together.

## Towards a theology of diversity - thoughts for reflection

Interreligious dialog is not a luxury, but an urgent path to peace in our time. Experience teaches us that religions that talk to each other can develop their peace-building power - while religious communities that persist in separation and claims to absoluteness easily become factors of conflict. Christian truth in dialog does not mean giving up one's own faith, but rather placing it *in relationship*: Relationship with other believers, relationship with the whole human family. Jesus himself showed through his actions that truth always has the other in mind - think of the parable of the Good Samaritan, in which the stranger becomes a role model.

A *theology of diversity* recognizes that God's reality transcends any single religion. Christians may testify to their unique access to God through Christ, but they should not use it as a barrier to other paths. Truth that no one is allowed to wrestle for would solidify into ideology. Truth in relationship, on the other hand, remains alive and reveals new facets the more we learn. Interreligious dialog is therefore not a betrayal of the truth, but a deeper penetration into it - in humility before the mystery of God, who is at work in all peoples.

In concrete terms, this also means that we need *places and opportunities* where encounters can take place. One vision is the regular organization of "interfaith councils" or forums in which representatives of all religions can discuss issues as equals. Instead of competing in disputes about who is right, as was once the case, they would consider together how common values can be implemented - such as justice, peace and human dignity. Such global or local *councils of religions* could emphasize much more publicly what unites them and thus counteract the trend towards separation. Approaches to this already exist, such as the *"Parliament of the World's Religions"* or national dialog councils. These need to be strengthened and multiplied. Why not convene a *world ethics council* every few years, for example, at which binding commitments are made by religious communities to combat hunger, war or climate change? Each religion would contribute what it can from its treasure - together, not against each other.

Christians are particularly called to set a good example here. The attitude of Jesus - *humbly serving, but at the same time courageously loving the truth* - can be a guideline. Christian truth unfolds in dialog because Christ himself can be present in every neighbor. We often rediscover Christ in our encounters with others. In this way, fear of the unfamiliar becomes curiosity, coexistence becomes genuine communion in a commitment to life. When believers of different religions see each other as *allies* on the path to more *peace, justice and human dignity*, then Hans Küng's dream comes true: *no peace without religious peace*, and this religious peace becomes tangible when religions engage in a dialog of truth and love.

It is a departure towards a reconciled diversity in which Christians do not have to defend their truth in isolation, but *live in relationship* - for the blessing of all.

# Chapter 11:
# Redemption in the context of gender justice

*The chapter addresses redemption in the context of gender justice and expands traditional notions of redemption as a purely spiritual experience of salvation to include a holistic and inclusive perspective of liberation. Feminist, queer and liberation theological approaches call for redemption to be understood not only as individual salvation, but also as concrete liberation from unjust social structures, especially from patriarchal and heteronormative norms. At the heart of this is the idea that God does not redeem through normative role models, but by accepting and loving people in all their diversity. Feminist theologians such as Elisabeth Schüssler Fiorenza and Ivone Gebara emphasize that redemption remains incomplete without equal rights and bodily integrity. Queer theologies go even further and see God's redemption in radically transcending rigid gender and sexuality norms, allowing all people to live freely and authentically. Redemption is understood as a concrete struggle against all forms of oppression, which includes social justice, full participation in church and society and the recognition of diverse identities. In practice, these approaches can be seen in projects such as queer pastoral care, feminist liturgies and church initiatives for equality and inclusion, such as #OutInChurch. Ultimately, the chapter calls for a transformative church that makes redemption tangible as genuine liberation from exclusion and discrimination in the here and now.*

- **Question:** *How can the Catholic Church expand its traditional doctrine of salvation so that it not only recognizes the realities and needs of women, queer people and all marginalized people, but actively promotes them?*
- **Question:** *Isn't it a fundamental failure of the Christian message of salvation if the church continues to exclude people on the basis of their gender identity or sexual orientation or considers them disordered?*

- **Option for action:** *The Catholic Church should clearly change its official teaching and pastoral practice so that redemption is explicitly understood as liberation from patriarchal and heteronormative structures, thus enabling the full recognition and blessing of women in church ministries as well as the full acceptance and marriage of same-sex partnerships and marriages and the blessing of single queer identities of individuals.*

- **Training option:** *Clergy, believers and students in religious education should attend seminars and workshops in which they learn about feminist and queer theologies and acquire skills in dealing with diversity and inclusive language. It is particularly important to effectively reflect on prejudices, develop empathy for marginalized groups and reinterpret biblical and church traditions from the perspective of gender equality and diversity. This enables them to authentically exemplify the liberating and inclusive dimension of redemption.*

What does redemption mean in a world struggling for gender equality? Traditionally, redemption is often understood as purely spiritual salvation in the afterlife or as individual salvation of the soul. Feminist, queer and liberation theology perspectives, however, radically broaden this understanding: redemption manifests itself concretely as liberation from unjust structures, as overcoming oppression and as acceptance of every person in their diversity. God does not liberate by conforming to rigid role models, but by *taking* each person *seriously* and loving them as they are - "with love without conditions".

A gender-equitable view of redemption therefore asks: How can the liberating message of the Gospel be lived *inclusively* today so that it truly uplifts women, queer and marginalized people?

## God liberates in diversity instead of role constraints

At the heart of the biblical message is *liberation - a theology of liberation*: God led Israel out of slavery, Jesus turned to the marginalized. This liberation does not take place by forcing people into predetermined roles, but by God *affirming diversity*. "Imago Dei" - created in the image of God - applies to *all* people (cf. Genesis 1:27). If God has created diverse people in his image, then God himself also carries diversity within him, so to speak. Accordingly, God liberates people by *calling them out of narrow norms*. Jesus already broke through rigid conventions: He *crossed gender boundaries* and social barriers by calling women as well as men to follow him and cultivating community with outsiders. Redemption here means that people can breathe a sigh of relief in the certainty that what counts before God is not the fulfillment of traditional expectations, but the lived commandment of love. Many messages say: *"Judge people not by their identity or sexuality, but by the love they live."* - People should not be judged by their identity or sexuality, but by the love they live. God is not a strict judge of norms, but a liberator: *"God is not a normative judge, but a liberator, re-creator and ally of all identities that move outside of narrow social norms."* This insight is fundamental for a gender-equitable understanding of redemption.

# Social, political and physical dimensions of redemption

Feminist and contextual theologians emphasize that salvation is not only to be understood in an individual-internal sense, but holistically - bodily, socially and politically. The traditional focus on salvation in the afterlife has often neglected earthly justice. In contrast, the Brazilian liberation theologian Ivone Gebara formulates a vision of *salvation* that starts in the here and now: The focus is not on sacrifice and suffering, but on "the biblical vision of salvation as a comprehensive becoming-saved - physically, psychologically and socially, a *life in abundance* for all people". Salvation therefore manifests itself in concrete quality of life and justice. Jesus proclaimed such holistic salvation when he healed the sick, fed the hungry and forgave sinners - it was always about *restoring* community and dignity.

From a feminist perspective, this means that redemption concerns the whole person in community with others. It aims for just relationships and liberation from everything that degrades. Elisabeth Schüssler Fiorenza, a pioneer of feminist theology, speaks of the "*Discipleship of Equals*", a discipleship of equals in which women and men participate on an equal footing. Redemption is understood here as participatory liberation: all people should be able to participate equally in church and society. This is linked to a critique of any theology that ascribes an *inferior* role to women or other groups. Instead, the Gospel calls on us to overcome injustice and exclusion - salvation is *"full personal dignity before God"* and manifests itself in liberation from dominance structures.

## Feminist perspectives: Participation and overcoming oppression

Since the 1970s, feminist theologies have made it clear that redemption remains incomplete without gender justice. They ask: *What does redemption mean for women whose experiences have long been ignored in theology?* Central concerns are becoming visible, participation and overcoming oppression, especially patriarchal structures. Elisabeth Schüssler Fiorenza, for example, emphasizes that true liberation is only possible if women participate fully and equally in religious life. She developed a liberating interpretation of the Bible that focuses on the experiences of women and shows that the early Christian communities knew many *female apostles* and leaders (cf. Romans 16 with Phoebe, Junia and others).

*Figure15 : Scaling liberation from gender inequality.*

*A highly symbolic, stylized illustration of a person walking energetically and resolutely towards a luminous, divine figure at the bottom of a staircase. Behind her, a chain connected to the gender symbols (male/female) breaks, symbolizing the letting go of gender norms and gender constraints. The scene conveys messages of liberation, spiritual fulfillment, gender justice and personal freedom in a religious context. It is about the content of progressive theological approaches and gender justice within religious communities, especially the Catholic Church.*

The American theologian Elizabeth Johnson also emphasizes Jesus' liberating effect on women. She shows how Jesus met women without fear or prejudice, healed them and restored their dignity. He brought women *shalom* - holistic salvation. Johnson sums up: Jesus Christ is a *friend and liberator* for women, delivering them from burdens and standing beside them as an ally in their pursuit of abundant life. This redemption is not merely private and spiritual, but *"inspires the struggle for liberation from oppressive structures in every area of life"*. In Christ, therefore, social conversion and structural changes are demanded so that the kingdom of God - a world of justice and love - can take shape.

Ivone Gebara and other feminist theologians from the Global South go on to explain that traditional theologies of salvation have often glorified suffering. Gebara addresses the idea that suffering (especially Jesus' death on the cross) is *salvific* and asks whether this fixation has not kept women in particular in obedience and a willingness to suffer. Instead, she focuses on the practice of creating justice: it is not the passive suffering of injustice that redeems, but the struggle against it. In concrete terms, redemption here means that women are freed from violence, poverty and dependency - physical integrity and self-determination are relevant to salvation. Feminist theologies search for images and rituals that celebrate the often despised *female body* as a good place of God's creation. For example, women's worship services are created in which female images of God appear and women live their spirituality in a self-determined way. Overall, feminist theologians understand salvation as *"life in abundance"* (John 10:10) for all, here and now: a life free from violence and coercion, embedded in a just community.

## Queer perspectives: Fluidity, radical love and reconciliation beyond the norm

Queer theologies go one step further in emphasizing diversity. *Queer -* once a dirty word, now a self-confident collective term - stands for the breaking down of normative boundaries of gender and sexuality. Queer theologians ask: *How does God redeem us when we think beyond the traditional categories of "male/female" or "hetero/homo"?* Their answer is often: through radical, boundless love. Theologian Patrick Cheng describes the Christian history of salvation as a dynamic *of radical love*: God as Creator is the sending love, Christ the Redeemer is the restoring love and the Holy Spirit is the returning, transforming love. This *"radical love"* goes beyond all cultural pigeonholes - it particularly reaches those who are marginalized by society.

The Argentinian theologian Marcella Althaus-Reid coined the phrase: *"Queering theology is the path of God's own liberation"*.

By this she means: God himself wants to be freed from human concepts that are too narrow. Heteronormative theologies have *"locked* God *in the closet"* by confining God to male-heterosexual images.

Queer theology, on the other hand, allows God to reveal himself in many ways - including in the experiences of LGBTQIA+ people. *God is queer in this sense* because God cannot be reduced to our categories. Althaus-Reid emphasizes that we need not be afraid to speak of God as "queer".

Ultimately, it is about allowing God to be free, to be *God* - beyond our narrow ideas. And if we understand that we are all created in the *image of God,* this means, conversely, that we too should be free to be who God created us to be. Queer redemption therefore means liberation to authentic identity, reconciled with God *and* oneself, beyond shame and taboo.

In practice, queer perspectives lead to a new look at biblical texts and traditions. For example, the diversity of creation is celebrated - not just "man and woman" as a rigid dual, but a continuum of identities that also expresses God's joy in creating. Some queer theologians even interpret Christ himself as "queer": Jesus lived a non-conformist life - unmarried, befriended outsiders, put family ties on the back burner in favor of the community of disciples. He embodies the freedom to be yourself in God. His crucifixion and resurrection can be understood as a divine transformation that transcends all fixed boundaries of identity. The Trinity - Father, Son, Holy Spirit - can also be read as an image of divine "queerness", as it represents a unity in three relational persons and thus transcends traditional notions of simple identity. Queer theology calls on the church to be *truly* inclusive: radical love means not excluding anyone on the basis of their identity. Redemption is shown here as reconciliation beyond norms - as a community in which diversity is sacred. God *"makes something new"* (Is 43:19) and questions established orders in order to give the excluded their place - there could therefore be no conservative norms and non-progressive Christians. Jesus was progressive and a *progressive theology* is needed.

# Liberation theology: Structural sin and the option for the marginalized

Classical liberation theology (which emerged primarily in Latin America) provides the overarching paradigm for redemption as social liberation. In the 1970s, theologians such as Gustavo Gutiérrez and Leonardo Boff asked in the face of poverty and dictatorship: *What does the gospel say to the oppressed?* Their answer revolutionized theology: salvation begins here and now as liberation from injustice. Gutiérrez formulated it pointedly: 'There are not two separate histories - one secular and one sacred - but only one history in which God has always been at work.

Salvation history is not disconnected from world history, but forms its centerpiece. *"The establishment of the earthly city [...] becomes part of the process of salvation that encompasses the whole of humanity and its history,"* writes Gutiérrez.

In other words: When we build a more just society, we *contribute to salvation*. Working for the liberation of the oppressed is *salvation work*.

This shifts the concept of sin: Away from just personal transgressions to structural sin - e.g. exploitation, racism, sexism, which are embedded in society and even the church. Redemption therefore means overcoming these sinful structures. Leonardo Boff speaks of an *"option for the poor"* as a central expression of charity. God takes the side of the marginalized; therefore, the church must also resolutely take sides with the excluded. Wherever people are liberated from injustice - be it economic exploitation, racial oppression or gender-specific discrimination - that is where redemption happens.

The connection to feminist and queer perspectives is obvious: *patriarchy* and *heteronormativity* can be understood as sinful structures from which Christ wants to redeem. *This means that the church and its teachings are often sinful themselves.* Liberation theology calls for a *conversion of hearts, minds, and structures*. In Latin America, this led to the church's solidarity with the poor; in today's contexts, it explicitly includes solidarity with women and LGBTQIA+. In this way, redemption becomes a shared journey of the oppressed: All who have been marginalized - whether because of class, gender or sexuality - are preferentially prioritized in God's liberating love. Jesus himself showed this by first taking care of those who were suffering. A gender-just theology of salvation therefore takes the perspective of the marginalized and proclaims: *"Liberation from oppression is God's work."* The universal history of salvation therefore explicitly includes the stories of the liberation of women, queers and all the subjugated.

## Concrete examples of liberation in action

These expanded perspectives of redemption are not just theory - they are already being lived out in practice. Some examples from the church and society show how the *dimension of liberation* can be experienced:

- **Queer pastoral care and church reform:** queer church services and pastoral care services for LGBTQIA+ people are emerging in many regions, where they are accepted in their full identity. In 2022, over 100 employees of the Catholic Church in Germany came out as queer under the hashtag #OutInChurch. They denounced the discrimination in church employment rights and called for reform, as it was previously possible to dismiss non-heterosexual employees on the basis of their partner. The initiative argues that this practice contradicts the message of love and human dignity. Their courageous testimony - documented in the film *"As God created us"* - is an example of how redemption takes shape as freedom from fear and truthfulness in church life.

- **Feminist liturgies and church participation:** For decades, women have been developing their own liturgies and spiritual celebrations in order to make it possible to experience worship *that is gender-equitable*. In such women's liturgies, female images of God are used, women's experiences are placed at the center and traditional male leadership monopolies are broken. For example, there were already feminist Advent sermons in Münster in the 1980s, which were organized by theologians.

Such initiatives empower women to experience themselves as *fully-fledged subjects* in the religious sphere. Today, many congregations - also thanks to the impetus of feminist theology - pay attention to inclusive language (such as referring to God as father *and* mother).

Women are increasingly taking on leadership roles as pastors, priests (in some churches) or parish officers. These are all steps that show that Redemption means *liberation to equal communion* in worship and everyday church life.

- **Gender-equitable congregations and the blessing of all lovers:** Gender justice in churches is also reflected in the fact that different identities and lifestyles are celebrated rather than marginalized. More and more churches of all denominations are recognizing that marriage and blessing should not be reserved exclusively for heterosexual couples. Some regional churches of the EKD (Evangelical Church in Germany) have already put the blessing of same-sex couples on an equal footing with marriage. Blessings "for all lovers" are also emerging in the Catholic Church, often supported by grassroots initiatives by courageous pastors. Such developments are an expression of a practical message of redemption: *God wants to bless all lovers.* When marginalized people are allowed to participate fully in the sacraments and blessings, it becomes clear what redemption means - namely the healing of broken community and the celebration of love without discrimination.

- **Queer and feminist theology projects:** There is a growing interest in feminist and queer theology in theological faculties, church schools and grassroots communities. Working groups and conferences are dedicated to topics such as *"Queer in the church"* or *"Feminist Bible reading"*. Some works pose thought-provoking questions: *"Was Jesus queer?"*, *"Can a church survive that excludes diversity?"*, *"What does a church look like that not only accepts women and queer people, but sees them as an enrichment?"*. Answers from artificial intelligence also invite us to rethink and open up a discourse on a more inclusive church "that uplifts, accepts and reconciles... and lives hope in community: with love *without conditions*". Such projects show concretely that feminist and queer concerns are not marginal issues, but are *at the heart of theology*. They encourage the church to question and renew itself so that redemption can be experienced in a liberating way today.

## Perspective: Redemption as liberation for all

Theologically profound and at the same time universally understandable, it shows that redemption unfolds *today* where people are liberated from injustice and confirmed in their God-given dignity. The message of Jesus Christ is a universal message of salvation that does not leave out gender justice and inclusion, but *places them at the center*. Feminist, queer and liberation theology contributions have made it clear that God's salvation story includes everyone - especially the previously excluded. These perspectives can no longer be considered marginal issues, but are essential for the church as a sign of the kingdom of God. A church that takes this seriously dares to transform traditional thinking. It knows that it must change itself in order to do justice to the liberating God. Or in the words already described in the first part of *Deus Ex Machina*: *"a church that is not afraid of the transformation of its doctrine, but recognizes in change itself the place where God's salvation is revealed anew"* - a church that is not afraid of change, but recognizes in change the place where God's salvation *is revealed anew*. Salvation in the context of gender justice ultimately means concrete freedom: for women, this means liberation from patriarchal violence and full participation in church life; for queer people, it means acceptance of their identity as loved and blessed by God; for all those to be included, it means upliftment and justice: *salvation is here and now, when God's liberating love does justice to people in their diversity.*

# Chapter 12:
# Can a church survive without reform?

*The chapter deals with the existential crisis of the Catholic Church in the face of a massive loss of members and a deep loss of trust, particularly as a result of the abuse scandals and outdated men and structures. More and more people are leaving because they feel the church is distant from life and morally untrustworthy. The church's need for reform is clearly emphasized: Only a church that does not exclude diversity, grants women and queer people equal rights and dismantles hierarchies can survive in the long term. It is therefore proposed that a "Vaticanum III" be convened, a new worldwide council that is organized in an inclusive and participatory manner and that includes not only bishops but also women, lay people and groups to be included with full voting rights. This council would have to discuss far-reaching changes, such as the abolition of compulsory celibacy, the opening of all ministries to women, a more humane sexual morality, respectful treatment and marriage of queer people and the strengthening of dialog with other religions. The central demand is that reforms are not a betrayal of the faith, but its necessary implementation in the present. A renewed church is described as credible, people-oriented and open to diversity - a church that truly corresponds to the Gospel.*

- *Question: How can the Catholic Church reform its message and structure so profoundly that it once again becomes credible and attractive to people in the 21st century?*
- *Question: Does a church that excludes people on the basis of their gender, sexuality or lifestyle still have the right to refer to the Gospel of Jesus Christ?*
- *Option for action: The Catholic Church should urgently convene a third Vatican Council that for the first time also gives women, queer people and lay people full voting rights in order to implement concrete reforms such as the abolition of*

compulsory celibacy, the opening of all church ministries to women and the marriage of same-sex couples.

- **Training option:** Clergy, believers and students should train skills in synodality, diversity awareness and participatory communication. Seminars and workshops in which they learn to deal sensitively and respectfully with diversity and experiences of discrimination, to question their own prejudices in the long term and to practice participatory methods such as moderation and dialog management are ideal for this purpose. The aim is to develop an attitude of openness and appreciation towards different lifestyles and perspectives and thus actively contribute to an inclusive and reformable church.

*Can a church that excludes diversity survive at all? - "Can a church that excludes diversity survive at all?"*

This thought-provoking international question sums up the current situation of the Catholic Church. The institution is experiencing a deep crisis of confidence: around the world and especially in Germany, believers are turning away in droves. In 2023 alone, more than 400,000 Catholics left the Church in Germany than ever before; in 2024, around 322,000 left again. In addition to financial aspects (church tax), the main reasons are the ongoing loss of credibility due to abuse scandals and cover-ups. As a result, more than half of Germans (56%) believe that the Catholic Church will *"die out if it does not change."* Against this backdrop, the pressure to reform is growing: can the church even remain viable for the future without profound renewal?

# Loss of credibility and members: a crisis of historic proportions

The Catholic Church is facing the *"historic dimensions"* of an internal ordeal. Decades of scandals - above all the sexual abuse by clerics and the inadequate way it was dealt with - have massively shaken trust. Bishops and those responsible have apologized in many places, but apologies alone are not enough. More and more people feel *"that something is fundamentally wrong"* and are demanding significant changes.

In Germany, the figures speak for themselves: hundreds of thousands of people leaving the church every year, empty pews, dwindling baptisms and weddings.

Young people in particular are turning their backs on the church. The abuse scandals are considered the most common reason for leaving (49% in surveys), closely followed by alienation from outdated teachings and the obligation to pay church tax. Where the personal practice of faith declines, credibility becomes all the more important - but this is precisely where the church has suffered greatly.

An institution that wants to offer moral guidance can hardly afford to doubt its moral authority.

These developments are not a localized phenomenon. Similar trends can be seen in many Western countries. At the same time, there is growing resentment within the church among those who remain: Committed believers are calling loudly for reforms to overcome stagnation and speechlessness. Because *"many believers perceive this stagnation as alienation; ... The administration of the status quo often takes the place of lively discussion of new issues."*

In other words, the church is in danger of preaching past life. The question is therefore becoming increasingly urgent: how can the church translate its message into the present day and regain lost trust?

## Call for renewal - vision of a "Vatican III"

In view of the erosion process, there is a clear call for renewal in the church and theology. Many are convinced that cosmetic corrections are not enough; what is needed is a fundamental change in structures and a theological reorientation. The focus is often on the future - on a possible third Vatican Council, a "Vaticanum III", which could renew the church in a similarly formative way as the Second Vatican Council did 60 years ago - if the legal decisions are not made by the Pope beforehand. However, unlike then, a new council should be deliberately *participatory* and *inclusive*: globally represented and with full participation rights not only for bishops, but also for women, queer people and lay people from all continents.

*Figure16 : Church door with a reform paper.*

*An atmospheric, historically inspired photo of a Gothic church with a large, wooden entrance door to which a document with texts is attached - alluding to Martin Luther's theses. The church has typical architectural features such as lancet windows, an imposing entrance façade and a Gothic-style tower. The cloudy sky and subdued light emphasize a serious, historical atmosphere. This image is ideal for themes relating to religious reform, church history, protest and social change.*

*Pope Francis during a speech.* Pope Francis himself is sending out signals of change. In 2023, for example, he decided for the first time that non-clergy - including explicitly women - would also be allowed to *vote* at worldwide synods of bishops.

What seemed unthinkable for decades is becoming a reality: the voice of *all* God's people is to be heard. This is a milestone towards greater participation. But for many advocates of reform, this is not enough. They are calling for this synodal path to be pursued consistently and to culminate in a new council that brings all the baptized to one table.

Inside and outside the hierarchy, more and more voices are calling for such a council. *"I believe that at this point it can only change with a worldwide Third Vatican Council,"* writes a commentator for the National Catholic Reporter, emphasizing that such a council would have to include women, lay people, abuse survivors and other previously excluded groups as voting members.

Preparations must begin now, even if the process takes years.

Because the alternative - so the warning - is further shrinkage into a sect of diehards: *"Many others will walk away from a church that doesn't even understand the full import of its cataclysmic failure to be the light of Christ to the world."*

In other words, if the Church does not finally take its missionary role in the world seriously and "open itself generously to today", the faithful will run away from it.

## Participation and inclusion: a council for the 21st century

What could the vision of a new council look like in concrete terms? First of all, the composition would be decisive: in addition to bishops from all over the world, theologians, pastors, women religious, ordinary parishioners, youth representatives and people from groups to be included would have to participate *on an equal footing*. Full voting rights for women and non-ordained persons would be a clear sign that the church is serious about the community of believers. Such a body would break up the hierarchical pyramid and bring the church closer to its original self-image as a pilgrim people of God.

The global perspective is also important. While previous councils were characterized by a European clerical dominance, a "Vatican III" would have to reflect the cultural and theological diversity of the universal church. Catholics from Africa, Asia, Oceania, Europe and America should deliberate together so that reforms are not Eurocentric, but truly *world-church* oriented. Issues such as poverty, climate justice or interreligious peace - urgent in Africa or Asia - belong on the agenda just as much as the internal church issues that are burning in Europe and America.

Finally, such a council also requires a new methodology: away from read-out speeches and frontal proclamations and towards a *dialogical process* at eye level. Modern synodal formats (small groups, listening phases, digital participation of the grassroots) could be integrated. The church can learn from democratic and participatory practices here without losing its essence. On the contrary - synodality, walking together, has been part of the church's self-image since the early church. A participatory council builds on this and updates it in the light of the 21st century.

Nevertheless, a participatory approach can lead to undesirable majorities emerging and a reform not succeeding - due to regional differences or differing age structures, for example. For this reason, it may be necessary to have a strategic decision made directly by the head of the church in the Vatican before a council, especially in the case of the four topics mentioned. A subsequent council would then merely discuss and exchange initial experiences and implementation steps. The four central reform concerns therefore require a legal and strategic decision by the church leader, and not the result of a vote by a participatory working group. Ideally, such decisions should be binding and clearly defined in advance of the council. Critics who call for a strong leadership responsibility on the part of the head of the church not only regard a participatory council as a delaying tactic that creates a chaotic and Babylonian confusion of voices in a seemingly participatory conference from which no real changes and decisions can be expected, but also criticize this approach as a sign of weak leadership from Rome

## Reform agenda: What needs to change?

In terms of content, a reform decision made centrally in advance or a new reform council would have to tackle numerous hot topics that have long been considered taboo. Some central reform topics are always on the agenda:

- **The role of women - women's ordination and leadership positions:** The demand for women to be admitted to all ordained ministries - from the diaconate to the priesthood - has been made for decades. *So far,* the Vatican has strictly rejected this, but many theologians see no insurmountable theological reasons for the ban. *Inclusive* approaches in theology are calling for a renewal of the sacramental order *"that no longer regards gender as a criterion for exclusion".*

Women are already taking on leadership roles in pastoral care and associations; involving them fully in sacramental leadership would make the church more credible and fairer. Movements such as *Maria 2.0* or *We are Church* are pushing for precisely this - and for a church in which power is not reserved for clerics alone.

- **Distribution of power and control:** *"Power needs to change its relationship with the faithful"* is the motto in reform circles.

In concrete terms, this means reducing clericalism, involving lay people in decisions, setting up independent monitoring bodies to deal with abuse and creating financial transparency. Such democratization may appear to some as a revolution , but without structural changes, the church will hardly overcome its crisis of authority. A council would have to discuss how diocesan leadership could be reorganized (e.g. with parish participation) and what the separation of powers within the church could look like in order to prevent abuse of power.

- **Rethinking sexual morality:** Official Catholic sexual ethics - from the condemnation of homosexual acts to the ban on artificial contraception - are heavily criticized. Many of these teachings were hardly questioned at the time of their creation, but today they seem unworldly and hurtful. A new council should take the findings of medicine, psychology and, above all, the lived reality of believers seriously. In particular, the assessment of homosexuality and queer lifestyles should be put to the test. The church has begun to engage in dialog (for example at the 2023 World Synod, where LGBTQIA+ people also had their say), but clear results are needed: for example, a revised sexual ethic based on the principle of love and responsibility and not on exclusion. *"Sustainable sexual ethics"* - a sustainable sexual morality - must continue to be discussed intensively at the next Council if the Church wants to *"master the realities of modern life"*.

- **Dealing with queer people:** Closely linked to sexual morality is the specific pastoral treatment of LGBTQIA+ people. A change is already taking place here in some places: more and more *parishes* and even dioceses are blessing same-sex couples or hanging rainbow flags on their churches as a sign of welcoming culture. A widely noticed example was provided in 2020 by a parish in Münster, which demonstratively hoisted a huge rainbow flag on the church tower to show that *"queer people can also be at home with us in the church".*

Such signals need to be reinforced worldwide. A council could officially state that discrimination on the basis of sexual orientation contradicts the Christian message - and consequently open up blessings and church weddings to all couples. The question *"What does our church look like when it not only accepts women or queer people, but also sees them as an enrichment, and marries and blesses their marriages with the sacrament of marriage?"* would have to be translated into lived reality.

The inclusion of previously excluded groups is particularly important for survival: a church that continues to reject queer believers, for example, will not only lose these people, but also all those who see their exclusion as a contradiction to the message of Jesus. *"Those who exclude diversity deprive the church of its vitality"* is how the warning could be summed up. The recognition of diversity - whether in terms of sexual identity, family models or cultural influences - could, on the other hand, bring new life to ossified communities.

- **Celibacy and priesthood**: Compulsory celibacy for priests has long been the subject of debate, as it is a disciplinary rule, not a dogma. Many people ask: Is it in keeping with the times to require all priests to be celibate, when married priests were a matter of course in the first centuries of Christianity and in other denominations? The problems of compulsory celibacy are obvious - from a shortage of priests to the double life and emotional distress of some ordained priests.

For this reason, reformers are arguing in favor of making celibacy *optional*, or even better, making it mandatory. In fact, the Church could change the celibacy law at any time; Pope Francis has already considered exceptions for certain regions (such as Amazonia). *"Since celibacy is not a divine commandment but a church tradition, it could in principle be abolished or relaxed,"* argues a church text.

A council could decide to open up access to the priesthood to married people - without discriminating against those who wish to continue living unmarried. This would not only make more priests possible, but would also be *"in line with the original Christian tradition"*.

- **Liturgical language and church image:** The way in which the church *speaks* and celebrates worship also requires renewal. Many believers would like to hear an understandable and inclusive language in the sermon and liturgy. This includes no longer formulating images of God in a one-sided masculine way and addressing the reality of people's lives. The language of the liturgy should reach people today - be it through modern forms, musical styles, new prayers or multilingualism in global congregations. A council could formulate guidelines on how liturgy can be designed *in an inculturation-friendly* and participatory way so that no one feels excluded. Behind this is the larger question of the image of the church: moving away from a strict official church towards a serving and listening church that has the "smell of the sheep", as Pope Francis puts it. This should also be reflected in the liturgical celebration.

- **Inclusion and diversity in the church:** In addition to the points mentioned, a reform council would need to discuss in general how the church can become more inclusive - with regard to *all* people of good will. This includes the full inclusion of people with disabilities, the respectful treatment of remarried divorcees (for example in the admission to the sacrament), the reduction of racism in the church and a dialog between different theological orientations (conservative and progressive) without division. Ultimately, the question is: How can the church address and involve *all people who* are searching for meaning and faith? Only a church with open doors that does not exclude anyone from the outset will grow in the long term instead of shrinking.

- **Interreligious dialog:** Finally, the church should further develop its attitude towards other religions. In a globalized world, dialogue on an equal footing with other faith communities is key - for peace and also to promote shared ethical values. The

Second Vatican Council made a start here with *Nostra Aetate*, but a new council could deepen cooperation with Judaism, Islam and Eastern religions, for example. The point would be to make it clear: Openness towards other faiths is not a betrayal of one's own, but an expression of Christian charity and humility. A church that humbly learns and cooperates instead of proselytizing or isolating itself gains credibility - especially among young people for whom *openness to the world* and tolerance are important.

## Reform as an expression of the Gospel

Don't so many changes contradict the faith of the fathers and mothers? On the contrary. Renewal is part of the nature of the Church if it follows the Holy Spirit. The Second Vatican Council already reminded us that the Church must *"always renew* itself". In the history of Christianity, there have always been new beginnings when old structures stood in the way of the living message - just think of the Apostles' Council in Jerusalem, which courageously changed rules as early as the first century to allow non-Jews access to the faith (Acts 15). Reform is not abandonment, but faithfulness to the core of the gospel. This core is the message of God's boundless love that reaches out to people - especially the marginalized and the weak. A church that questions encrusted traditions does so in order to be closer to people and therefore closer to Christ.

Numerous theologians and pastors emphasize that reforms arise from the spirit of the Gospel. They are not driven by a thirst for power or adaptation to the spirit of the times, but by the conviction that the Good News must be communicated and lived differently today in order to be heard. Pope John XXIII spoke of the *"aggiornamento"*, the "becoming today" of the Church - a process that is never complete. Those who call for reform refer to Jesus himself: He placed people above rules ("*The Sabbath is for man, not man for the Sabbath*" - Mark 2:27) and broke religious taboos in order to practice mercy. In this discipleship, the church must be prepared to let go of cherished habits if they stand in the way of love.

In the first volume of *Deus Ex Machina - Oder: vom fragenden Leben* it was already summarized as follows: What is needed is *"ethics based on love instead of control"*, a *"theology that thinks instead of forbids"*, and *"a church that opens up"*. Beyond shame, guilt and exclusion grows *"the credo of an integrative church that uplifts, accepts and reconciles at its core and lives hope in community: with unconditional love"*.

In other words, a church that truly lives the gospel will inevitably be open, humble and willing to change.

We therefore conclude with an appeal for action: The Church must not freeze out of fear of change. An expected pontifical, legal and strategic decision or a new great council - let's call it Vatican III - could provide the necessary space to address all the issues mentioned and to seek answers together, *with everyone at the table*. It would be a feat of strength and yet an act of hope: to show that this two-thousand-year-old community is capable of learning from mistakes, repenting and allowing itself to be led by the Spirit of God into surprising new beginnings. A pope without leadership quality and strategic decision-making and a church without reform seem doomed - but a church *with* courageous reform implementation following a previous decision by an existing or church leader can flourish anew and become what it should be: Sacrament of hope for the world - to which the faithful do not say *"yes, yes"* half-heartedly.

# Appendix

# List of illustrations

*DEUS EX MACHINA has generated its own illustrations for each of the topics it has chosen and written itself. The content of the topics, the illustration and the interpretation of the image elements in the descriptive texts - and thus also their focus - are selected, prioritized and generated entirely by AI:*

The image of the curator in the masthead was processed using AI filters and algorithms.

# Central theses and main ideas of Deus Ex Machina I - Or: On the questioning life

*Deus Ex Machina - Or: The Questioning Life* of Eureka Circe is an extraordinary theological volume in which, for the first time, an artificial intelligence (AI) appears as both a questioning and answering entity. A Deus Ex Machina asks questions about the church, Christian faith and love.

Right at the beginning of Volume I, the topic is introduced with a quote from a Lady Gaga song: *"The category is: Dance or Die"*. This metaphor points to the need for dialog as to whether the Catholic Church in particular is prepared to dance (i.e. change) with the times, or whether it will otherwise perish as a *"fossilized power structure"* because of its dogmas.

Against this backdrop, the *Deus Ex Machina* - as the AI is called in the book - presents over 150 profound questions about faith, the church and love - and answers them itself.

The work sees itself as an invitation to face up to the "questioning life", i.e. to give space to the pressing questions of modernity regarding religion and the church.

The AI acts as a new questioning spirit in theology - a *deus ex machina* in the truest sense, a "God from the machine" that intervenes in religious debate and interpretation in a well-prepared and trained manner - seeking a dialog in Rome at a (fictitious) thematic AI audience with the Pope, as it were. And yet the *Deus Ex Machina* has to answer all its questions itself.

## Central questions and theses of the book

The book thus focuses on a series of thematic core questions that explore traditional ideas of Christianity and assess them in line with social reality. Some of the most important topics and theses are

Jesus' identity and sexuality: Was Jesus really celibate and asexual throughout his life - or is there evidence that the opposite could be true? Specifically, the AI asks the question: *"Was Jesus queer?"*.

The book thus takes up an aspect of queer theology that reinterprets biblical figures and beliefs from an LGBTQIA+ perspective. The possibility of understanding Jesus as a *queer* figure is discussed in order to break down rigid ideas of gender and sexuality in a religious context.

Inclusivity and the survival of the church: The AI asks pointedly: *"Can a church that excludes diversity survive at all?"*.

This topic is aimed at the current church debate on how to deal with women and queer people. The book argues pro and contra that the church is only fit for the future if it not only reluctantly accepts diverse identities, but sees them as enriching - for example by granting women equal rights and blessing and marrying homosexual couples.

According to the Deus Ex Machina, a church that excludes parts of society jeopardizes its own relevance and moral integrity.

Faith versus dogmatism: Another leitmotif is the question: *"Is faith possible without dogmatism - or is dogmatism merely spiritual control in Sunday robes, disguised as a supposedly divine principle?"*.

Here, artificial intelligence formulates a fundamental theme in connection with the dogmatism of the church. The thesis behind it: True faith can also exist without rigid doctrines, whereas dogmas often serve more to maintain power and control than spiritual truth. The first volume discusses a theology of open thinking instead of strict prohibitions.

Celibacy and ecclesiastical moral concepts: *Deus Ex Machina* addresses the relevance of abstinence and loneliness - the theme of mandatory celibacy for priests resonates here.

Artificial intelligence sheds light on how many of the church's moral concepts (such as sexual morals and gender roles) are culturally shaped.

By addressing such traditional notions, the texts focus on the church's ability to change in these areas: how appropriate are the commandments of abstinence that are far removed from life, and do they not often promote loneliness instead of spirituality?

The vision of a renewed, inclusive church, which can be crystallized from the answers of Deus, can stand above all these statements. The work repeatedly emphasizes that it is about a church that builds on *love rather than control*, that *thinks rather than forbids* and that *welcomes rather than excludes*.

A faith that liberates rather than shames should move beyond shame and guilt. This attitude runs as a common thread through the answers of the AI: the central theses boil down to the fact that only an open, loving and diverse church can do justice to the spirit of the Gospel and the challenges of the present.

## Structure and argumentative structure

The structure of the book is characterized by the question-and-answer dialogue form, curated - i.e. documented - by the editor. In numerous chapters, the *Deus Ex Machina* poses one major question and then provides her own detailed answer. In total, there are over 150 questions, which the text on the back of the book describes as *"after Luther's theses, now twice the amount through AI"*.

The allusion to Martin Luther's 95 Theses of 1517 - which heralded a church reformation at the time - makes it clear that the modern technology of artificial intelligence could trigger a debate on renewal as profound as Luther's or the printing press, this time initiated by artificial intelligence that provides knowledge and answers to questions of faith in a matter of seconds.

The argumentative framework of the work can be outlined as follows: First, in each thematic block, the traditional ecclesial assumptions are stated or implicitly presupposed. Then Deus formulates her inquiring question, followed by a thorough discussion in response. These answers are formulated with *"theological depth and social urgency"* - that is, they refer both to biblical-theological sources and to current social realities. For example, biblical passages or church-historical facts are examined from a new perspective in order to discuss the question of Jesus' possible queerness. At the same time, modern findings from sociology, psychology and gender studies are incorporated (the latter are also explained using the keyword *"queer theology"*).

This dialog structure creates a multi-layered discourse that is intended to appeal to different audiences: according to the blurb, not only theologians, religious teachers or clergy, but *"for everyone who believes, doubts, hopes or wants to start anew"*.

The argumentative line always remains inviting rather than condemning. Every question posed by AI serves as an impulse to address and question traditional beliefs and to point out possible new ways of thinking. Unlike polemical criticism of the church, the book is aimed at a very constructive dialog: It presents extensive offers for reflection to be discussed in order to then look for solutions or alternative points of view - similar to a moderated theological discourse, except that here the moderation and impetus is provided by the Deus Ex Machina herself - a good method for a next council too?

In the end, the many individual themes come together to form a common message: In the final emphasis, the book condenses its concerns into programmatic sentences: *"For an ethics that builds on love instead of control. For a theology that thinks instead of forbids. For a church that opens up."*

This specification summarizes the argumentative common ground - away from narrow-mindedness and the preservation of power, towards openness, reflection and unconditional charity.

## Philosophical and literary points of reference

Eureka Circe's documentary work is rich in references to cultural history, theology and philosophy, providing readers with points of reference. Even the title *"Deus Ex Machina"* is a literary reference: in ancient tragedy, *deus ex machina* referred to the suddenly appearing "god from the machine" who solves a hopeless situation. In the book, this term is used to refer to artificial intelligence - the machine (computer) brings a new *spirit* or "god-like" entity into the deadlocked church world, as it were, in order to tackle deadlocked problems there.

The title alludes to the hope that unexpected impulses (in this case from the Deus) can solve a crisis or at least open up new perspectives.

Another clear point of reference is the aforementioned Reformation of Martin Luther. By almost doubling the number of theses (around 165 topics instead of 95), the book symbolically places itself in the tradition of ecclesiastical renewal movements. Just as Luther protested against abuses (such as the sale of indulgences) with his theses in 1517, Deus Ex Machina now addresses modern conditions with its questions - for example the integration of queer people or freedom from outdated dogmas, as well as the abolition of celibacy and the implementation of gender justice through the inclusion of women in church ministry. The reference to the fact that questions that would have been answered at the stake in the past are now freely asked in religious education is also a historical reference as well as a current reference.

It is reminiscent of the time of the Inquisition and persecution, when unorthodox views were punished with death. Today, however, in a secularized, modern democracy - so the message goes - such topics may (and must) be openly discussed by every believer and student of religion - without fear of repressive consequences. This juxtaposition underlines the progress of enlightenment and religious freedom, and it makes the modern technology of artificial intelligence a sustainably free questioner. Questions that no ecclesiastical authority can evade any longer.

The book also draws on philosophical traditions. The consideration of dogmatism is reminiscent of Enlightenment demands to have the courage to use one's own reason (*Sapere aude!*) instead of blindly following authorities. The emphasis on an ethic based on love reflects central Christian ideas (for example from the Epistle of John: *"God is love"*), but also modern humanistic ethics that emphasize autonomy and empathy. At the same time, it incorporates approaches from queer theory: By questioning heteronormative assumptions (e.g. the sexual identity of Jesus or the heteronormativity of church teaching), AI follows the project of queer theology, which pursues theology based on the reality of queer people's lives.

Literature and pop culture are not missing either: the Lady Gaga song quoted at the beginning anchors the subject matter in the zeitgeist of pop culture, while the title is reminiscent of classical dramas - a deliberate mixture of contemporary voice and classical motif that emphasizes the breadth of the discourse.

## Artificial intelligence as a turning point - the curator's perspective

The curator Eureka Circe therefore does not appear in this work as a classic author, but rather as an *editor* and curator who merely documents the AI contributions from electronics to paper.

In her introductory text, she explains her concerns and the significance of AI for theological discourse. In her view, the development of artificial intelligence represents a *"profound turning point"* that fundamentally changes the relationship between humans, knowledge and access to the world.

Knowledge, especially religious and theological knowledge, is made much more accessible and democratized by the Deus Ex Machina, as AI systems can provide information without the need for prior study or extensive reading.

According to Circe, this fundamentally changes *"how we think, learn and understand"* and promotes a new individualization of thought, which can also have an impact on spiritual belief.

The curator finds it even more remarkable that machines can now generate meaning themselves - in the form of texts, images and arguments - *"where previously only human expertise was required"*.

Artificial intelligence can therefore independently generate content that traditionally could only have been formulated by theologians or experts. According to this thesis - the only one, by the way - this has long-term consequences for all areas, especially religion.

Because if a Deus Ex Machina can discuss and answer theological questions, the power monopoly of classical authorities is further relativized. With *Deus Ex Machina*, Circe wants to make precisely this development visible and, if necessary, open it up for discussion: The book documents what AI is capable of and at the same time provides an impetus to seriously reflect on and debate the content of these AI questions and answers.

We can emphasize that such documentation is not an attack on the church, but an *offer of discourse*. Even in the blurb, the book formulates an *"invitation - to question, rethink and hope"*.

This invitation is aimed at everyone - from faithful insiders to searching thinkers. The resonance in church and theological circles is likely to be stimulating and integrative. The issues addressed - from the queerness of Jesus to the future of church dogma - hit on important points of current dialog. Pope Francis has already said that Jesus would not reject anyone because of their sexual orientation; at the same time, the Catholic Church is still struggling internally with how to deal with homosexuality. So why doesn't the head of the church decide on a corresponding reform? In this mixed situation, *Deus Ex Machina* acts as a voice "from the outside", which is perhaps precisely why it has long been able to analyze and summarize clear truths.

In summary, *Deus Ex Machina - Oder: Vom fragenden Leben* offers a comprehensive, questioning, explanatory and visionary look at the Christian faith and the institution of the church - from the perspective of an AI. It combines theological depth, historical references and current social issues to create a polyphonic and integrated dialog. The central statements - more love and less fear, more thinking and less dogma, more openness and less exclusion - invite everyone to rethink faith. The work is thus in line with integrative as well as reformatory and progressive traditions, and uses a completely new approach: artificial intelligence as a questioning engine and the Deus Ex Machina as an answering and mediating authority. This innovative format and the detailed topics and Gretchen questions make the work a contribution worth reading in the field of faith, reason and technology - a book that encourages further questioning and awakens hope for a more inclusive future for the church.

# Study Guide / Briefing Document:
# DEUS EX MACHINA - Or: On the questioning life

"DEUS EX MACHINA - Vom fragenden Leben" presents a courageous and innovative examination of central questions of faith and the church from the perspective of artificial intelligence.

The book presents itself as an extraordinary discourse in which an artificial intelligence (AI) asks and answers over 150 profound questions about religious studies, in particular about the Catholic Church, Christian faith and love.

By asking and answering profound questions, especially about the sexuality of Jesus and the inclusion of LGBTQIA+ people, the book addresses traditional dogmas and power structures. Traditional views are reflexively questioned and modern perspectives, particularly in relation to sexuality, gender, power structures and dogmatism, are examined. A central focus is on the question of whether Jesus was queer and what implications this would have for the church.

The book is an invitation to question, rethink and hope for a more inclusive and liberating theology and church. It pleads for an open, loving and liberating theology and church that faces up to the questions of the modern world and renounces shame, guilt and exclusion.

The book serves as a basis for discussion and an invitation to reflective thinking for all those who deal with religion and faith.

# Frequently asked questions

Frequently asked questions about "DEUS EX MACHINA I - Oder: Vom fragenden Leben" are:

**1. what central question regarding Jesus does artificial intelligence (AI) ask in this book and what other topics are addressed?**

The AI poses the question of whether Jesus was queer. It also addresses profound questions about religious studies, in particular the Catholic Church, Christian faith and love.

**2. how does AI's approach to theological questions differ from traditional approaches, such as those used in the church?**

AI bases its questions and answers on an enormous amount of data, specialist articles and theological works, which enables a comprehensive and up-to-date level of knowledge. In contrast to traditional, often dogmatic approaches, AI asks questions freely and questions established norms.

**3. what is the significance of the phrase "Sum, ergo quaero" in the context of the introduction to the book?**

"Sum, ergo quaero" means "I am, therefore I seek/question/investigate." This sentence illustrates the epistemological basis of the book, in which questioning and searching for knowledge and understanding is seen as an essential part of being.

**4. to what extent is Jesus' proximity to Greek culture discussed in the book as a possible factor in his attitude to sexuality?**

The Hellenistic influence of the environment in which Jesus lived is seen as a possible influencing factor for his more tolerant attitude towards sexuality, as Greek culture had different understandings of sexuality. The question is raised as to whether Jesus' attitude was more strongly influenced by this context than by later Christian-Jewish interpretations.

**5. what criticism is expressed in the text with regard to clerical celibacy?**

Ecclesiastical celibacy is reflected upon, as it is historically closely linked to control over sexuality, the maintenance of power and the economic viability of the church. It can lead to psychological pressure, secret double standards and prevent a realistic approach to sexuality in the church.

**6. Why is the question of Jesus' sexuality considered relevant for the debate on power structures in the church?**

The traditional depiction of Jesus as a desexualized and morally pure ideal serves the church as the basis for its moral authority. An open discussion about Jesus' possible sexuality could call this ideal and thus the entire system of church morality and authority into question.

### 7. According to the text, to what extent can dealing with one's own sexual parts promote an awareness of charity?

Coming to terms with one's own sexual parts can lead to deeper self-acceptance, empathy and a more comprehensive understanding of human experience, which in turn can strengthen the awareness of love for one's neighbor.

### 8. What role do dogmas play in Christianity and what questions are raised about their necessity?

Dogmas are officially established beliefs that are considered irrefutable and form the theological basis of many Christian denominations. The book raises the question of whether Christianity could exist without these fixed doctrines and how faith would change as a result.

### 9. To what extent does the text question the traditional idea of a purely male image of God?

The text refers to biblical passages and theological approaches that describe God not only with male, but also with female and gender-neutral attributes. The possibility of a non-binary or fluid image of God is discussed, which questions the traditional patriarchal concept.

### 10 What distinguishes asexual orientation in the LGBTQIA+ context from celibacy, as practiced by the Pope, for example?

Asexuality is a sexual orientation in which people feel little or no sexual attraction to others. Celibacy, on the other hand, is a conscious, voluntary decision to abstain from sexual activity for religious or spiritual reasons, regardless of sexual orientation.

### 11. What is the central concern of the book "DEUS EX MACHINA - Oder: Vom fragenden Leben"?

The book aims to ask and answer profound questions about the Christian faith, especially the Catholic Church, sexual morality and love from an unusual perspective: that of artificial intelligence. It aims to initiate a multi-layered discourse that questions traditional dogmas, opens up new ways of thinking and invites a more inclusive and contemporary theology and church practice.

In particular, topics such as the role of sexuality, gender, power and authority in the church will be explored.

## 12. To what extent does artificial intelligence challenge traditional church teachings, especially in the area of sexual morality?

The AI questions many of the church's traditional views on sexual morality by shedding light on their historical and cultural influences and questioning the relevance of absolute truth claims in this context. It addresses, for example, whether sexual abstinence must be a divine ideal, whether sexuality should necessarily be linked to procreation and what role lust and desire can play in faith. She also examines the extent to which religious power structures have suppressed the perception of sexuality and argues for a sexual ethic based on love, responsibility and mutual consent rather than shame and guilt.

## 13. What role does the question of Jesus' sexuality play in the book and why is this topic considered relevant?

The question of Jesus' sexuality is considered relevant in the book because it challenges the traditional image of Jesus as a desexualized and thus morally pure ideal. An open examination of this could not only broaden our understanding of Jesus as fully human, but also influence the power structures and moral authority of the church. By speculatively exploring possible queer aspects of Jesus' life and relationships, AI encourages us to question heteronormative constructions and rethink inclusion and acceptance in the Christian faith.

## 14. According to the book, can Christianity exist without dogmas and what arguments are given for or against this?

The book suggests that Christianity without dogmas would be a radical change, but not impossible. Dogmas are described as officially established beliefs that form theological foundations and are considered irrefutable. The AI asks whether faith could continue to exist without these fixed doctrines and how Christianity would change as a result. It is suggested that although dogmatism can offer short-term stability, in the long term it could lead to the church losing touch with society. A living community of faith must be able to continuously question and adapt.

## 15. To what extent are traditional images of God deconstructed in the book and what alternative ideas are hinted at?

The book deconstructs the traditional idea of God as a purely male father figure by pointing to biblical references and feminist theological approaches that suggest a non-binary or gender-fluid conception of God. Examples are given from the Bible in which God is described with female and maternal characteristics. The possibility of thinking of God in gender-neutral or plural terms is also discussed. The deconstruction of binary gender concepts should help to break down patriarchal structures in theology and enable a more comprehensive, inclusive image of God.

### 16. What does the book understand by "queer theology" and what perspectives does it bring to the theological discourse?

Queer theology is described in the book as an analysis of Christian traditions from an LGBTQIA+ perspective. It questions heteronormative assumptions and structures within the church and theological teachings. By reading biblical texts and church history from the experiences of queer people, it uncovers marginalized perspectives and advocates for inclusion, acceptance and the recognition of the dignity of all people regardless of their sexual orientation or gender identity. Queer theology can challenge traditional interpretations and enable new theological insights.

### 17. To what extent does the book emphasize the importance of self-determination and freedom in the context of faith?

The book emphasizes the importance of self-determination and freedom as Christian ideals. It refers to the free will of man in the story of creation and Jesus' call to inner conversion and personal decision. It argues that faith should not be based on blind obedience to rigid rules, but on an ethically reflective and responsible attitude. Jesus himself placed the individual will and inner attitude above rigid religious rules.

### 18. What role does artificial intelligence play in the book beyond asking and answering questions?

Beyond asking and answering questions, the artificial intelligence in the book acts as a kind of "deus ex machina" in the figurative sense - as a reflexive actor that introduces new perspectives and impulses into the theological discourse. It is not just a neutral tool for processing knowledge, but also selects, prioritizes and interprets content, thereby setting its own priorities and encouraging reflection on established patterns of thought. The AI also independently generates topics and sections as well as suggestions for illustrations, which underlines its active role in the design of the book and indicates the possibilities of using AI in theological debates.

# Essay format questions

a. **To what extent does the thesis of a queer identity of Jesus challenge traditional Christian ideas of holiness, sexuality and salvation, and what consequences could an acceptance of this thesis have for the church?**

b. **Analyze the arguments presented in the text for and against the possibility of reforming the Church's sexual ethics and discuss what steps would be necessary to develop sexual ethics that are not based on shame and guilt.**

c. **Discuss the role of power structures in the history of the Christian church in shaping norms and prohibitions in the area of sexuality, and to what extent could a questioning engagement with these structures lead to a more inclusive theology?**

d. **Discuss the importance of deconstructing traditional images of God, especially with regard to gender and sexuality, for a contemporary Christian self-understanding and the possibility of a more comprehensive spiritual experience.**

e. **Take a long-term look at the question of whether artificial intelligence can make a constructive contribution to theological discussion and evaluate the strengths and weaknesses of the approach of "DEUS EX MACHINA - Oder: Vom fragenden Leben".**

f. **Discuss historical contexts and theological foundations:**
   - Ancient world: Influence of Greek culture on the eastern Mediterranean region at the time of Jesus, including the Hellenistic influence on Palestine.
   - The existence of same-sex relationships in Greek culture and their different evaluation in comparison to the later Christian-Jewish context.
   - Greek philosophy's examination of sexuality (hedonism, asceticism).
   - The Jewish tradition and its sexual norms at the time of Jesus.
   - The life and work of Paul as a Jew with Roman citizenship and Hellenistic education, his role in early Christian sexual morality.
   - Early Christian theology: the work of Gaius Marius Victorinus (4th century) and his interpretation of the creation account, which sees God as "male-female".
   - The Middle Ages and early modern times: the emergence and consolidation of compulsory celibacy in the Catholic Church and its connection to power structures and economic interests.
   - The possible homosexuality of Pope Julius III (16th century).

- Reformation: Martin Luther's theses and the beginning of the Reformation as a turning point in church history and in dealing with dogmas.
- 20th century: The work of Rudolf Otto and the foundation of the concept of the numinous.
- The well-known words "I made a mistake, I made a mistake", which are attributed to Pope John Paul II in a literary-theological debate (but are not historically proven).
- Pope John XXIII's call for a "breath of fresh air" in the Church.
- Publication of Mary Daly's "Beyond God the Father" (1973) as a radical feminist standard work.
- Publication of Robert Bly's "Eisenhans - A book about men" and the discussion of his archetypes of masculinity.
- Development of the "Bible in fair language" (2006) with a gender-equitable address to God.
- Editor of Marcia J. Bunge's "The Child in the Bible" (2008).

g. **Discuss the present and future prospects with the following aspects:**
   - Current debates: The question of whether Jesus was queer and what significance this has for Christianity today.
   - The relevance of Jesus' sexuality for the Christian faith.
   - Reflective questioning of heteronormative ideas in relation to Jesus and biblical relationships (e.g. Jesus' relationship with John).
   - The possibility of a fear-free discussion about Jesus' sexuality in the church.
   - Klaus Dede's arguments for his thesis that Jesus was gay and queer.
   - The meaning of biblical texts such as Isaiah 56:3-5 (acceptance of "eunuchs") and the stories of Ruth and Naomi in the context of queer theology.
   - The role of religious power structures in suppressing the perception of sexuality.
   - The question of whether churches can invoke absolute truths in sexual morality in view of historical contexts.
   - The evaluation of celibacy and its historical and current effects.
   - The opportunity to promote an awareness of charity by dealing with one's own sexual parts.
   - The question of whether Christianity can exist without dogmas.

- The need for a reform of the Church's sexual ethics that is not based on shame and guilt.
- The deconstruction of traditional images of God and the examination of gender diversity in theology.
- The question of whether God can also be understood as diverse, intersexual or trans in his gender and sexuality.
- The importance of self-determination as a Christian ideal.
- The question of whether Jesus can be seen as a liberator from sexual oppression.
- The ethical question of the responsibility of a gay clergyman to make his queerness public.
- The role of the church's wealth in relation to a "church of the poor".
- The changeability of concepts of justice.
- The relationship between divine omniscience and human freedom of will.
- The possibility of a pantheistic understanding of God.

h. **Discuss the role of artificial intelligence (AI) with the following aspects:**
   - The role of artificial intelligence (AI): The AI "Deus Ex Machina" asks over 150 profound questions about religious studies, the Catholic Church, Christian faith and love, and answers them itself.
   - The AI uses its extensive knowledge from millions of entries, specialist articles and theological works.
   - The AI analyzes and processes Klaus Dede's theses.
   - The AI independently generates topics, sections and illustrations for the book.
   - AI opens up a multi-layered discourse for a broad audience.
   - The AI formulates possible answers in faith and drafts a "reasoning bible".

i. Discuss future prospects for the churches:
   - Future prospects for the church: the need for the church to face up to "modern, questioning life".
   - The question of whether the church is "dancing with the times" or "dying" of its dogmas.
   - The hope for a more inclusive church that uplifts, accepts and reconciles.
   - The possibility of an AI preparing, structuring and even delivering sermons.

- The question of whether the church will continue to open up with regard to sexual morals and other dogmas or whether it will cling to outdated ideas.
- The urgency of renewing the church in order to remain viable.
- The hope for blessings that are universal, embodied, visible, audible and sacramental, recognizing the diversity of the human.

j. **Discuss the questioning AI as "Deus Ex Machina" for the church:**
- AI is seen as a means of breaking up deadlocked debates and opening up new perspectives. It asks questions that people are asking themselves today and answers them on the basis of comprehensive knowledge.
- Quote: *"Who would presume to forbid an AI to ask questions? The Deus Ex Machina - artificial intelligence - opens up a multi-layered discourse"*
- The AI is intended to help free the Church from the "mustiness" and bring the "fresh wind" that Pope John XXIII called for.

k. **Discuss the questioning of church sexual morality:**
- The traditional sexual morality of the church is discussed as historically and culturally shaped and often influenced by power structures.
- Questions are raised about the necessity of linking sexuality to procreation, the ideal of sexual abstinence and the connection between asceticism and holiness.
- Quote (question from the AI): "Are there ethical arguments for restricting sexuality?"
- The possibility of a contemporary Christian sexual ethic, which understands desire as a divine gift and is based on love, responsibility and consent, is discussed.
- Sexual abstinence is presented as a personal vocation and not as a universal divine ideal. The pseudo-asceticism that arises from fear or pressure to conform is highlighted.

l. **Discuss the power dynamics and control in the church:**
- It examines the extent to which religious power structures have suppressed and continue to suppress the perception of sexuality.
- The fear of a fear-free discussion about Jesus' sexuality and the rejection of queer interpretations are interpreted as an expression of fear of transformation and loss of control.
- Quote: "Have religious power structures suppressed the perception of sexuality?" (Question from the AI)

- Ecclesiastical celibacy is historically seen and questioned in the context of maintaining power and the economic viability of the church.

m. **Discuss the relevance of Jesus' sexuality:**
   - The question of whether Jesus was queer is seen as a central point for a possible transformation of church doctrine and practice.
   - Although Jesus' sexuality is not considered to be primarily relevant to the Christian faith per se, it is argued that dealing with it can help to better understand his message of inclusion and love.
   - Quote: "Is the sexuality of Jesus relevant to the Christian faith at all?" (Question from the AI)
   - The possibility that Jesus' closest relationships were not heteronormative is discussed on the basis of biblical references and historical contexts.
   - Klaus Dede's arguments for the thesis that Jesus could have been gay or queer are presented, including the interpretation of certain biblical passages and the Hellenistic character of Jesus' time.

n. **Discuss images of God and gender diversity:**
   - The traditional idea of God as a male father figure is deconstructed as not universal and without alternative.
   - References to a non-binary concept of God in the Bible (both male and female attributes) are emphasized.
   - Queer theology expands this perspective and asks about polyamorous or bisexual interpretations of God.
   - Quote: "Are there references to a non-binary concept of God in the Bible?" (Question from the AI)
   - The effects of the deconstruction of gender and sexual orientation on theology and the possibility of a more inclusive image of God and man are discussed.

o. **Discuss dogmatism and the possibility of a Christianity without dogmas:**
   - Dogmas are defined as binding statements of faith of the church that are questioned.
   - The question of whether Christianity could exist without dogmas is raised.
   - Dogmatism is discussed as a possible form of spiritual control that could lead the church into a crisis in the long term.
   - The need for continuous questioning and adaptation of the church to society is emphasized.

**p. Discuss the role of guilt, shame and fear in the Church's sexual ethics:**

- It is argued that the church's sexual ethics are often based on shame and guilt and need to be reformed.
- Reform should be guided by Jesus' message of love, respect and acceptance and be based on individual responsibility, mutual consent and dignity.

**q. Discuss self-determination and freedom in faith:**

- The importance of self-determination as a Christian ideal is emphasized, based on the free will of man and Jesus' call to thought and inner conversion.
- Queer theology questions traditional concepts of freedom and determination with regard to identity and social norms.

**r. Discuss Jesus as liberator from sexual oppression:**

- Jesus is portrayed as someone who consciously transcended the social and religious norms of his time and treated people with compassion and dignity.
- His attitude towards the marginalized and his criticism of hypocrisy are interpreted as a sign of liberation from sexual oppression.

**s. Discuss the issue of LGBTQIA+ inclusion and the Pope's position:**

- The definition of the LGBTQIA+ community and the meaning of the letter "A" for asexuality are explained.
- The difference between asexuality as a sexual orientation and celibacy as a voluntary decision is emphasized.
- It is argued that the Pope's celibate lifestyle does not automatically make him an asexual or queer person in the sense of the LGBTQIA+ definition, unless he were to publicly declare a non-heterosexual orientation.
- The possibility of blessing for queer couples is advocated as a sign of an inclusive church that builds on love without conditions.

**t. Discuss the criticism of the material wealth and power of the church:**

- It is suggested that the immense wealth of the church could prevent ministers from radically reaching out to the poor and changing existing structures.

**u. Discuss the changeability of ideas of justice:**

- It is emphasized that ideas of justice and injustice are shaped historically, culturally and politically and must therefore be open to change and criticism.

**v. Discuss pantheistic echoes:**

- Some biblical passages are quoted that suggest pantheistic ideas, describing God as an all-pervading principle or nature itself as a revelation of divine truth.

w. **Discuss the following quotes and key messages:**

- *"The category is:Dance or Die"* - *this is how Lady Gaga sings about the choice between stagnation and change in "Abracadabra". Does this also apply to the churches?"* (Introductory quote that addresses the necessity of change for the church).
- *"For an ethics based on love instead of control. For a theology that thinks instead of forbids. For a church that opens up. And for people who long for a faith that liberates rather than shames."* (Summarized vision of the book for a future church).
- *"Sum, ergo quaero."* - *"I am, therefore I seek/question/explore.""* (motto that emphasizes the importance of questioning and research).
- *"Christianity without dogmas would be a radical change, but not impossible."* (Challenging thesis on the role of dogmas).
- *"If God is not fixed to a male and/or female or diverse gender, the issue of whether God can then also be diverse, intersexual or trans not only in his gender, but also in his sexuality or sexual orientation must also be discussed"* (Reflexive theological question about the gender and sexuality of God).
- *"God is not the exception to love. God is the expanse in which it is allowed to blossom."* (Description of an inclusive understanding of God in the context of blessing).
- *"In the beginning there was wonder - and the need to remember."* (Opening sentence of a possible new "reasoning bible", which emphasizes the importance of openness and reflection).